# LANGUAGE
## UNLEASHED

Unveiling the Future of Communication
and Information Retrieval

Laura Walker

© Copyright 2023 - All rights reserved.

The content contained within this book may not be reproduced, duplicated or transmitted without direct written permission from the author or the publisher.

Under no circumstances will any blame or legal responsibility be held against the publisher, or author, for any damages, reparation, or monetary loss due to the information contained within this book, either directly or indirectly.

**Legal Notice:**

This book is copyright protected. It is only for personal use. You cannot amend, distribute, sell, use, quote or paraphrase any part, or the content within this book, without the consent of the author or publisher.

**Disclaimer Notice:**

Please note the information contained within this document is for educational and entertainment purposes only. All effort has been executed to present accurate, up to date, reliable, complete information. No warranties of any kind are declared or implied. Readers acknowledge that the author is not engaging in the rendering of legal, financial, medical or professional advice. The content within this book has been derived from various sources. Please consult a licensed professional before attempting any techniques outlined in this book.

By reading this document, the reader agrees that under no circumstances is the author responsible for any losses, direct or indirect, that are incurred as a result of the use of information contained within this document, including, but not limited to, errors, omissions, or inaccuracies

# TABLE OF CONTENTS

Introduction .................................................................................... 1

**Chapter 1: Foundations of Language** ......................................... 3
    Historical Perspectives on Language ........................................ 3
    The Neurobiology of Language .................................................. 6
    Language Acquisition and Development ................................ 11

**Chapter 2: The Digital Language Revolution** ............................ 18
    Rise of Digital Communication ................................................ 18
    Social Media and Language Evolution .................................... 23
    Impact on Traditional Communication Channels .................... 28

**Chapter 3: Natural Language Processing (NLP)** ....................... 36
    Understanding NLP .................................................................. 36
    Applications in Everyday Life .................................................. 42
    NLP's Role in Information Retrieval ........................................ 47

**Chapter 4: AI and Language** ..................................................... 53
    Conversational AI ..................................................................... 53
    Language Models and Their Impacts ....................................... 57
    AI and Personalized Communication ...................................... 63

**Chapter 5: The Future of Linguistic Technology** ...................... 69
    Emerging Technologies in Linguistics ..................................... 69

Augmented Reality and Language ............................................ 75
Potential Innovations on the Horizon ...................................... 80

## Chapter 6: Language and Human Connection ........................... 86
Impact of Technology on Human Interaction ......................... 86
Maintaining Authentic Communication .................................. 91
Overcoming Challenges in the Digital Age ............................. 96

## Chapter 7: Ethical Considerations in Language Unleashed ....... 104
Privacy Concerns ..................................................................... 104
Bias in Language Technology ................................................. 109
Responsible Development and Use of Language Tools ......... 114

## Chapter 8: Language Unleashed in Education .......................... 119
Transforming Language Learning ........................................... 119
AI in Education ........................................................................ 122
Future Perspectives on Linguistic Education .......................... 125

## Chapter 9: Beyond Language: Multimodal Communication ..... 129
Visual and Auditory Communication ...................................... 129
Integrating Multimodal Approaches ...................................... 132
Impact on Information Retrieval ............................................ 136

## Chapter 10: Navigating the Uncharted Territory ...................... 140
Challenges and Opportunities ................................................ 140
The Role of Society in Shaping Language Unleashed ............. 144
Envisioning the Next Phase of Linguistic Evolution ................ 148

## Conclusion ................................................................................. 153

## Introduction

Welcome to "Language Unleashed: Unveiling the Future of Communication and Information Retrieval," a groundbreaking exploration into the evolving landscape of human language and its transformative impact on how we communicate and access information. In a world where language is the cornerstone of connection and understanding, this e-book embarks on a journey to unravel the possibilities that lie ahead.

Language, the most ancient means of human expression, is leading the way in technological innovation as it develops at a rate never seen before. "Language Unleashed" invites you to navigate the linguistic horizon where traditional communication converges with cutting-edge developments, reshaping how we interact, share ideas, and retrieve information.

The introduction sets the stage by addressing the dynamic nature of language in our contemporary world. We explore the symbiotic relationship between language and technology, examining how artificial intelligence, natural language processing, and other emerging technologies reshape communication. The communication landscape is undergoing a paradigm shift from voice-activated assistants to language-driven algorithms.

This e-book peels back the layers of conventional language use, revealing the potential of emerging trends and technologies. We delve into the promises and challenges posed by machine learning, linguistic algorithms, and the fusion of language with data analytics. "Language Unleashed" turns into a manual for comprehending how these developments fundamentally transform information retrieval in addition to improving human communication.

As readers embark on this journey, they are encouraged to envision the future of language, where communication barriers are transcended and information is seamlessly accessible. "Language Unleashed" is a call to inquiry for everyone who wants to learn more about and use language's power in this exciting time of technological upheaval. Explore the future of information retrieval and communication, where language can run wild.

# Chapter 1

# Foundations of Language

**Historical Perspectives on Language**

Studying language is like taking a trip down memory lane, discovering the rich fabric human expression has woven over thousands of years. To truly understand the languages we speak today, we must delve into the historical perspectives that have shaped their evolution. Our linguistic heritage is a testament to humanity's ingenuity, adaptability, and cultural richness.

The origins of language are veiled in the mists of prehistory, and theories regarding its emergence abound. One hypothesis posits that language evolved gradually, with early humans developing complex communication systems to coordinate group activities. A different explanation proposes a rapid and profound event, possibly a genetic mutation, that gave our ancestors the ability to speak. Regardless of its genesis, the emergence of language marked a watershed moment in our species' history.

The historical development of language reveals ancient civilizations as crucibles of language evolution. The Sumerians, nestled between the Tigris and Euphrates, left an indelible mark on linguistic history with the creation of the world's first known writing system – cuneiform. This wedge-shaped script, etched onto clay tablets, captured the spoken word in a tangible form, laying the foundation for recorded language and literature.

The Greeks improved in the skill of expression as they moved westward. Because of its elegance and clarity, classical Greek was used to communicate philosophy, science, and the arts. The works of Homer and the philosophical musings of Plato and Aristotle not only showcased the linguistic prowess of the Greeks but also laid the groundwork for the development of grammatical theories and linguistic analysis.

Rome, with its vast empire, was a melting pot of languages. The language of the Roman aristocracy, Latin, was essential to government and administration and the dissemination of Christianity. The influence of Latin on the Romance languages is evident today, as French, Spanish, Italian, Portuguese, and Romanian share linguistic roots with this ancient tongue.

The Middle Ages witnessed the proliferation of vernacular languages, spoken by ordinary people, alongside Latin. The emergence of epic poems like "The Song of Roland" in Old French and Geoffrey Chaucer's "The Canterbury Tales" in Middle English reflected the shift towards embracing local languages for literary expression. This period saw linguistic diversity blossoming and language's gradual democratization.

The Renaissance marked a revival of classical learning and a renewed interest in the structure and beauty of language. Humanist scholars like Erasmus and the polymath Leonardo da Vinci celebrated linguistic expression as an art form. This era laid the groundwork for developing dictionaries and grammatical treatises as scholars sought to codify and standardize languages.

During the Age of Exploration, European powers delved into unexplored regions, broadening language boundaries. Contact with indigenous languages in the Americas, Africa, and Asia introduced novel words and linguistic influences, enriching the lexical tapestry of European languages. Concurrently, the global exchange of goods and ideas facilitated linguistic borrowing and adaptation, shaping languages in unforeseen ways.

A period of reason and intellectual ferment began with the Enlightenment. Philosophers such as John Locke and René Descartes pondered the nature of language and its role in shaping thought. The foundation for linguistic theories that would later impact the growth of structural linguistics and contemporary linguistic theory was established during the Enlightenment.

In the 19th century, we witnessed the rise of historical linguistics, spearheaded by scholars like Sir William Jones and Franz Bopp. Comparative analysis of Indo-European languages revealed shared linguistic roots, giving birth to the concept of a linguistic family tree. Additionally, ancient writings such as Jean-François Champollion's Rosetta Stone were deciphered during this period, which offered insights into long-lost languages.

In the 20th century, linguistics underwent a paradigm shift with the advent of structuralism and, later, generative grammar. Structural linguistics, championed by Ferdinand de Saussure, focused on the inherent structure of language and its internal relations. Noam Chomsky's generative grammar introduced the idea of universal grammar, suggesting an innate, biological basis for language acquisition.

The digital age has brought about unprecedented changes in language dynamics. The internet, a global network connecting diverse linguistic communities, has given rise to new forms of communication and linguistic evolution. Emojis, acronyms, and abbreviations have permeated online conversation, upending preconceived ideas about language and communication.

In conclusion, historical perspectives on language offer a panoramic view of our linguistic heritage, from the mysterious origins of communication to the digital age's dynamic linguistic landscape. Each epoch has contributed to the rich mosaic of languages we encounter today, reflecting human expression's ingenuity, adaptability, and cultural diversity. Understanding historical linguistic trajectories provides us with a perspective through which to view language's lasting strength and resilience over time as we negotiate the complications of modern communication.

## The Neurobiology of Language

The complexity of language, which is a hallmark of human intellect, is closely linked to the complex processes occurring within the brain. Comprehending the neuroscience of language reveals an intricate web of brain pathways, cognitive functions, and physiological systems supporting our communication ability. The brain, an instrument of unmatched complexity that composes the language symphony of expression and comprehension, is at the center of our investigation.

The foundational elements of language processing are rooted in the brain's structure and organization. Broca's area, which is situated in the left frontal lobe, and Wernicke's area, located in the left temporal lobe, are both essential regions related to their respective functions of language production and comprehension. The discovery of these specialized language areas dates back to the 19th century when Paul Broca and Carl Wernicke made groundbreaking observations of language deficits in patients with specific brain lesions. The subsequent elucidation of Broca's area as responsible for syntax and grammar and Wernicke's area for semantic processing marked a pivotal moment in understanding the neurobiological foundations of language.

Language processing extends beyond these discrete areas, involving a network of interconnected regions across the brain. There is a bundle of nerve fibers known as the arcuate fasciculus. Linking Broca's and Wernicke's areas facilitates communication between language-related regions. Advanced researchers can now visualize the dynamic interplay between these regions during language tasks. This networked approach underscores the distributed nature of language processing, emphasizing the collaborative efforts of various brain regions.

The journey into the neurobiology of language explores the macroscopic structures and the microscopic intricacies of neural communication—the basic building blocks of the nervous system, were neurons exchange messages electrochemically. The connections between neurons, or synapses, are essential for transmitting these impulses. Chemical messengers called neurotransmitters allow information to pass across synapses. The complex interplay of neurotransmitters, receptors, and ion channels orchestrates the intricate dance of neural communication that forms the basis of language processing.

Recent developments in neuroimaging technologies have equipped researchers with the ability to investigate language processing in real-time, providing insights into the temporal dynamics of neural activity. Event-related potentials (ERPs) and magnetoencephalography (MEG) offer millisecond-level resolution, unveiling the rapid succession of cognitive events during language tasks. This temporal precision has revealed the cascading nature of language processing, where different neural processes unfold in a synchronized sequence, from phonological analysis to syntactic parsing and semantic integration.

Language acquisition, a hallmark of human development, further unveils the dynamic interplay between genetics and environmental influences in shaping the neurobiology of language. Infants exhibit a remarkable capacity to discern linguistic patterns from an early age. According to the crucial period hypothesis, a window of opportunity exists for children to acquire language characterized by neuronal plasticity and flexibility. Genetic influences highlight the complex interaction between biology and the environment in forming our language abilities. One such gene is the FOXP2 gene linked to language development.

The structure and function of the brain change as people learn and use language. The bilingual brain exemplifies the remarkable adaptability of neural circuits in response to linguistic demands, providing a window into the broader spectrum of neurobiological plasticity.

The interaction between language and memory further enhances our knowledge of the neuroscience of language. Language, inherently linked to memory, engages the hippocampus while encoding and retrieving linguistic information. The intricate dance between language and memory is evident in the nuances of word recall, sentence construction, and the retention of linguistic patterns.

Beyond the confines of spoken and written language, the neurobiology of language extends to non-verbal communication and the processing of symbolic representations. Gesture comprehension, for instance, involves integrating visual and linguistic information in the brain. The mirror neuron system, a network implicated in both action execution and observation, contributes to our ability to understand and interpret gestures, facial expressions, and other non-verbal cues. In written language, recognizing letters, words, and symbols activates complex brain networks refined via literacy and schooling, demonstrating the neurological foundations of symbolism.

Language disorders, such as aphasia, apraxia, and dyslexia, provide critical insights into the neurobiology of language by highlighting the specific disruptions in neural circuits. Aphasia, often resulting from damage to Broca's or Wernicke's areas, manifests as difficulty in language production or comprehension. Speaking apraxia manifests as a lack of coordination of the necessary motor movements for speaking, highlighting the complex relationship between language expression and motor control. Dyslexia, a reading disorder, underscores the role of neural circuits in visual processing and phonological awareness.

The neurobiological exploration of language extends beyond individual cognition to the social dynamics of communication. The social brain hypothesis posits that the evolution of larger human brain sizes is linked to the complexities of social interactions, including language-based communication. From the nuances of conversational turn-taking to the interpretation of social cues, the neurobiology of language intertwines with our innate social nature.

The advent of neuroimaging has opened new frontiers in the study of language disorders and their rehabilitation. Researchers can see the brain alterations linked to language recovery in aphasic patients receiving therapy thanks to functional MRI. These developments highlight the possibility of using neurobiologically guided treatments to address linguistic impairments and encourage healing.

In conclusion, the neurobiology of language is a multidimensional exploration that weaves together the macroscopic and microscopic intricacies of the brain. From the specialized language areas of Broca and Wernicke to the distributed networks of interconnected regions, from the electrochemical signaling of neurons to the adaptive plasticity of neural circuits, the neurobiological underpinnings of language underscore the remarkable complexity of human cognition. As technology advances, providing ever more sophisticated tools for probing the mysteries of the brain, our understanding of the neurobiology of language will undoubtedly deepen, unraveling new layers of insight into the intricate dance between the mind and language.

**Language Acquisition and Development**

Language acquisition and development constitute a remarkable journey that defines the essence of human communication. From the moment a child utters its first words to the sophisticated linguistic expressions of adulthood, this process is intricate and awe-inspiring. The mechanisms via which people, especially newborns, learn and internalize language are the subject of language acquisition research. In contrast, the more comprehensive idea of language development includes the lifetime development of linguistic skills. Understanding these processes involves unraveling the intricate interplay between nature and nurture, cognitive processes, and social interactions.

The foundations of language acquisition are laid during infancy, a period marked by rapid cognitive development. Theories of language acquisition highlight the interplay of genetic predispositions and environmental stimuli. The nativist perspective, epitomized by Noam Chomsky's Universal Grammar theory, posits an innate linguistic template hardwired into the human brain. This perspective holds that children naturally communicate through language, which is developed through exposure to linguistic stimuli. Chomsky's emphasis on the universality of grammar across languages implies a shared biological blueprint that facilitates language acquisition.

In contrast, the empiricist perspective, championed by behaviorist B.F. Skinner emphasizes the role of environmental influences in shaping language development. Skinner proposed that language is a learned behavior acquired through operant conditioning, reinforcement, and imitation. His theory implies that linguistic competence is shaped by external factors, such as parental feedback and environmental stimuli, rather than an innate linguistic blueprint. The nature-nurture debate around language acquisition reflects the continual effort to determine the relative contributions of heredity and environment in forming linguistic ability.

As infants enter the world, they are immersed in a rich auditory environment, exposing them to language's cadence, rhythm, and phonetic diversity. The perceptual narrowing phenomenon, observed in the early months of life, suggests that infants initially exhibit a broad sensitivity to the sounds of all languages but gradually narrow their focus to the phonetic nuances specific to their native language. This narrowing indicates the brain's adaptive responsiveness to linguistic input, honing in on the significant sounds in the child's environment.

Developing phonological awareness and the ability to discern and manipulate language sounds is a pivotal milestone in language acquisition. Infants begin by discriminating between speech sounds and distinguishing phonetic contrasts relevant to their native language. The foundation for later phonemic awareness—the capacity to identify and operate with the tiniest acoustic units that carry meaning—is laid by this phonetic sensitivity. Phonemic awareness is crucial to reading and spelling acquisition, demonstrating the complex relationship between spoken language and literacy development.

The verbal developmental milestones attained in the first year of life are remarkable. Babbling, the repetitive production of consonant-vowel combinations, emerges around six months, allowing infants to experiment with the sounds of their native language. By the end of the first year, infants transition from babbling to producing their first words. The one-word or holophrastic stage marks the beginning of intentional communication, as infants use single words to convey various meanings.

The expansion of vocabulary during the second year reflects the emergence of the two-word stage, characterized by simple combinations of words. These word pairings, which are frequently telegraphic, express fundamental syntactic connections without fully formed grammatical structures. The explosion of vocabulary and the onset of grammatical development during this period indicate the child's increasing mastery of language structure and complexity.

Theories of syntactic development provide insight into how kids pick up the conventions of sentence construction. Jean Piaget's cognitive-developmental theory posits that cognitive maturation precedes linguistic development, with children acquiring linguistic structures as their cognitive abilities advance. In contrast, the behaviorist perspective, exemplified by the work of Skinner, emphasizes the role of reinforcement and imitation in shaping syntactic development. The interactionist approach synthesizes these perspectives, highlighting the bidirectional influence of cognitive maturation, environmental input, and social interaction in shaping syntactic skills.

Developing semantic understanding, or the meanings conveyed by words and sentences, is an intricate aspect of language acquisition. The overextension phenomenon, where a child applies a comment to a broader range of objects than adults, is a common feature of early semantic development. Over time, children refine their semantic understanding, forming more precise associations between words and their referents. The acquisition of word meanings involves not only the mapping of sounds to objects but also an understanding of the relationships between terms and the contexts in which they are used.

It is impossible to overestimate the importance of social interaction in language development. The sociocultural theory, pioneered by Lev Vygotsky, posits that language development is inherently tied to social interaction and cultural context. Language acquisition is scaffolded through social interactions within the ZPD, where adults and peers provide linguistic input and support that exceeds the child's independent capabilities.

Caregiver-infant interactions significantly influence language development, particularly the quality and quantity of language input.

The linguistic input hypothesis, proposed by linguist Stephen Krashen, suggests that exposure to comprehensible language input slightly beyond the child's current linguistic abilities promotes language acquisition. Studies that show a correlation between the richness of early language input and later language competency and cognitive results highlight the significance of responsive and engaging interactions.

As children progress through preschool, language development becomes more nuanced, reflecting the refinement of syntactic, semantic, and pragmatic skills. The social use of language, or pragmatics, includes the norms around nonverbal cue interpretation, turn-taking, and discourse. Understanding social context, being aware of conversational conventions, and modifying language use for various communication partners are all necessary for developing pragmatic abilities.

The shift to formal education brings new possibilities and obstacles to language development. Literacy skills, built upon the foundation of oral language, become a focal point of educational endeavors. The alphabetic principle, the understanding that written symbols represent the sounds of spoken language, forms the basis for learning to read and write. Acquiring literacy skills involves integrating phonological awareness, phonics, vocabulary, fluency, and comprehension.

The bilingual advantage hypothesis suggests cognitive benefits for bilinguals, including enhanced executive functions and metalinguistic awareness. Bilingualism presents a dynamic interplay of linguistic systems, requiring individuals to navigate between languages based on situational and contextual cues. The cognitive flexibility that bilingualism honed demonstrates the human brain's adaptation to linguistic diversity.

Language development extends into adolescence and adulthood, reflecting the dynamic nature of linguistic abilities across the lifespan. The development of metalinguistic awareness—the capacity to consider and evaluate words—contributes to the sophistication of language. Adolescents engage in abstract thinking, allowing for the exploration of complex linguistic structures and rhetorical devices. The process of acquiring academic language, distinguished by specific vocabulary and discourse conventions, is becoming increasingly evident as people move through formal educational settings.

The study of language development intersects with various disciplines, including psychology, linguistics, education, and cognitive science. Longitudinal research endeavors, tracking individuals from infancy to adulthood, provide valuable insights into the trajectory of language development and its correlates with cognitive, academic, and socioemotional outcomes. Multidisciplinary viewpoints, encompassing fields such as cognitive neuroscience and sociolinguistics, enhance our comprehension of the intricate aspects of language acquisition.

In conclusion, language acquisition and development constitute a multifaceted journey that begins in infancy and unfolds across the lifespan. A complex interplay of genetic predispositions, environmental factors, cognitive processes, and social interactions shapes language development. From the emergence of babbling in infancy to the refinement of metalinguistic awareness in adolescence, language development encompasses a continuum of milestones and challenges. The study of language acquisition and development deepens our understanding of human communication's intricate processes. It informs educational practices, interventions for language disorders, and our appreciation of the diverse linguistic landscapes shaped by individual and cultural experience

# Chapter 2

# The Digital Language Revolution

**Rise of Digital Communication**

Unquestionably, digital communication has changed how we communicate, connect, and interact. This seismic shift, driven by technological advancements, has not only revolutionized the speed and reach of communication but has also redefined the very nature of human connection. As we navigate the intricate digital communication landscape, it becomes imperative to explore its historical roots, examine its profound impact on various aspects of society, and critically assess the challenges and opportunities it presents.

The genesis of digital communication can be traced back to the mid-20th century, with the advent of the electronic computer. The development of early computing machines laid the groundwork for creating digital communication technologies. An important turning point was reached in the 1960s with the launch of ARPANET, the forerunner of the contemporary internet. Unintentionally, this government-funded effort that sought to build a decentralized communication network resistant to nuclear strikes opened the door for the democratization of knowledge and the advent of the digital age.

The evolution of digital communication gained momentum with the creation of email, a transformative tool that revolutionized how people exchange messages. In addition to streamlining professional communication, email's ease of use and effectiveness ushered in a new era of personal interaction. The advent of the World Wide Web in the early 1990s further democratized access to information, enabling users to publish and consume content globally. This democratization made possible the participative culture that defines modern digital communication.

The rise of social media platforms in the 21st century has been a defining chapter in the narrative of digital communication. Platforms like Facebook, Twitter, Instagram, and LinkedIn have become integral to the fabric of social interactions, enabling users to connect, share, and curate their digital identities. Social media has made it possible for people to communicate with people who have similar interests, regardless of where they are physically located. The power of social media in shaping public discourse, mobilizing social movements, and disseminating information has made it a potent force in the digital age.

Citizen journalism, blogging, and user-generated content have democratized the creation and distribution of news. While this democratization has empowered individuals to share diverse perspectives, it has also raised concerns about the reliability and integrity of information. The "fake news" phenomenon and the ease with which misinformation can spread in the digital realm underscore the challenges associated with democratizing information.

Digital communication has not only altered how we access information but has also redefined the nature of interpersonal relationships. The immediacy of communication facilitated by messaging apps, video calls, and social media has collapsed temporal and spatial barriers, enabling real-time interactions across the globe. But this continual connectedness has also brought forth new difficulties, such as privacy concerns, digital exhaustion, and the fuzziness of personal and work spheres.

One of the profound impacts of digital communication is its role in shaping contemporary culture. Memes, hashtags, and viral phenomena have given rise to a new vocabulary of cultural expression. People now actively participate in the production and distribution of cultural content thanks to the height of the digital sphere. Platforms like YouTube, TikTok, and podcasting have democratized content creation, allowing individuals to become creators and influencers in their own right.

A paradigm shift has also occurred in the business landscape due to the proliferation of digital communication. E-commerce, digital marketing, and online advertising have become central to the success of businesses in the digital age. How companies interact with customers has been revolutionized due to the capability to communicate with a worldwide audience, target particular demographics, and adjust marketing plans based on user data. However, this digitalization of commerce has raised concerns about data privacy, cybersecurity, and the ethical implications of targeted advertising.

The educational sector has witnessed a digital revolution by integrating technology into learning environments. E-learning platforms, online courses, and digital collaboration tools have expanded access to education, allowing learners to engage with educational content from anywhere in the world. The pandemic brought about an additional acceleration of the adoption of digital communication tools in education, which brought to light both the benefits and the challenges associated with distant learning.

Even with the many benefits of digital communication, it's critical to acknowledge and deal with the problems that come with it. Disparities in access to technology, or the "digital divide," continue to be a significant global problem. Socioeconomic factors, geographical location, and infrastructural limitations contribute to uneven access to digital resources, exacerbating existing inequalities.

The effect of internet communication on mental health is another urgent issue. The constant connectivity, the pressure to curate a positive online image, and the addictive nature of social media have been linked to increased levels of stress, anxiety, and depression. Cyberbullying, online harassment, and the adverse effects of excessive screen time further underscore the importance of fostering a healthy digital culture that prioritizes well-being.

In the digital age, privacy degradation is a divisive topic that has to be carefully considered. The collection and utilization of personal data by tech companies for targeted advertising and algorithmic decision-making raise ethical questions about consent, autonomy, and surveillance. Finding a balance between the advantages of customized services and the defense of personal privacy is a difficult task that calls for constant social dialogue and legislative frameworks.

When we consider how digital communication has grown, it's clear that its influence goes beyond information and technology. It has reshaped communication, transformed cultural dynamics, altered business models, and redefined educational paradigms. Digital communication is not merely a tool but a pervasive force permeating every facet of contemporary society.

Digital communication has both promise and uncertainty for the future. The ethical considerations surrounding data privacy, the regulation of digital platforms, and the social implications of constant connectivity will continue to be critical areas of discourse.

In summary, the emergence of digital communication marks a turning point in human history. This evolution has been revolutionary, from the humble origins of electronic computing to the omnipresence of social media and the complexities of contemporary digital culture. As we navigate the opportunities and challenges of the digital age, we must approach digital communication critically, mindful of its far-reaching implications on individuals, societies, and human connection.

## Social Media and Language Evolution

Social media has ushered in a new communication era, profoundly impacting language's evolution. The dynamic interplay between digital platforms and linguistic expression has given rise to a rich tapestry of linguistic innovations, challenges, and cultural shifts. The complex relationship between social media and language evolution is examined in this article, which also looks at the historical context, investigates linguistic phenomena specific to digital communication, and considers the wider societal ramifications of this revolutionary convergence.

Social media's influence on language evolution is deeply rooted in the historical trajectory of digital communication. Websites facilitating social networking, such as Friendster and MySpace, began in the early 2000s; they established the groundwork for a paradigm shift in how individuals interact with online language. But the emergence of Facebook, Twitter, Instagram, and other modern platforms thrust social media into the mainstream and created an atmosphere where language is evolving at a never-before-seen rate.

One distinctive feature of social media language evolution is the brevity imposed by character limits. With its 280-character constraint, platforms like Twitter have catalyzed the emergence of new linguistic forms. The compression of language, driven by the need to convey messages concisely, has given rise to abbreviations, acronyms, and novel word forms. Words like "OMG" (Oh My God), "LOL" (Laugh Out Loud), and "ICYMI" (In Case You Missed It) have become ubiquitous in digital discourse, shaping an abbreviated and efficient mode of communication.

The hashtag, originally a functional symbol used to categorize content, has evolved into a linguistic phenomenon transcending social media. Using hashtags, denoted by the '#' symbol, allows users to participate in more extensive online conversations, link related content, and contribute to trending topics. The hashtag has become a linguistic marker of cultural and social movements, playing a role in shaping public discourse and influencing linguistic trends beyond the digital realm.

The concept of virality, inherent in social media dynamics, has introduced new dimensions to language evolution. Catchphrases, memes, and neologisms can spread quickly among a wide range of internet audiences thanks to a viral article, video, or meme. The speed and scale of this dissemination contribute to the rapid integration of new linguistic elements into the vernacular, shaping linguistic trends and expressions.

Emojis are visual symbols used in Internet communication to represent ideas, feelings, and reactions. Emojis are a prime example of the visual turn in digital communication, where nonverbal cues can enhance or even wholly replace text. Emojis offer subtle expressiveness that enables users to express context, tone, and emotion in a condensed visual format. The widespread use of emojis is a prime example of how language is changing to accommodate different forms of communication.

The linguistic landscape of social media extends beyond written text to include multimedia elements. Memes—funny pictures or videos with reader added—have become a popular form of expression. The meme format, characterized by its shareability and adaptability, allows users to engage in cultural commentary, satirical humor, and social critique. The rapid circulation of memes contributes to the evolution of language by encapsulating cultural references and linguistic twists within visual and textual elements.

The participatory nature of social media platforms, where users actively contribute to content creation and dissemination, fosters a linguistic ecosystem shaped by user-generated content. Blurring traditional roles between content producers and consumers leads to collaborative language creation. Users can co-create linguistic content on social media through collective storytelling, language-based games, and hashtag challenges, among other activities.

Slang and colloquial expressions thrive on social media, becoming linguistic markers of online communities and subcultures. The diverse user base, each with unique linguistic practices and cultural references, contributes to creating niche vocabularies. Online communities frequently add slang, inside jokes, and terminology unique to their communities' lexicons. This phenomenon exemplifies how social media facilitates the formation of digital subcultures with distinct linguistic characteristics.

Despite the linguistic innovations spurred by social media, concerns about linguistic homogenization have been raised. Influenced by popular influencers, trending content, and platform algorithms, the prevalence of specific linguistic forms can contribute to language standardization. Pursuing virality may lead to a preference for linguistic elements that resonate with a broad audience, potentially overshadowing linguistic diversity and regional nuances.

Social media has become a locus for linguistic experimentation, challenging traditional grammatical norms and fostering a more fluid and dynamic language. Memes, hashtags, and user-generated content frequently exhibit purposeful deviations from standard spelling and grammar, demonstrating a lighthearted and imaginative approach to language. This linguistic flexibility, characterized by intentional misspellings, linguistic playfulness, and the blending of languages, challenges prescriptive language norms and expands the expressive potential of language.

Social media communication's immediacy and real-time nature contribute to the accelerated pace of language evolution. New words, expressions, and linguistic phenomena can quickly emerge and gain widespread usage. The ephemerality of trends, fueled by the rapid turnover of content on social media feeds, adds a temporal dimension to language evolution, with linguistic elements rising to prominence and fading into obscurity at an accelerated rate.

Social media has made it easier for everyone to have linguistic influence by giving them a voice in language conversation and trends. Influencers, content creators, and ordinary users contribute to linguistic innovation, with the potential to introduce new words or expressions that resonate with a broad audience—the fluid and decentralized nature of linguistic influence on social media challenges traditional gatekeepers and language authorities.

The symbiotic relationship between social media and language evolution extends beyond linguistic considerations to encompass broader societal impacts. The digital public sphere, facilitated by social media platforms, has become a space for public discourse, activism, and negotiating cultural norms. Hashtags, linguistic campaigns, and digital activism highlight the potential of social media to shape narratives, challenge power structures, and amplify marginalized voices.

However, democratizing linguistic influence on social media also raises ethical considerations. The dissemination of false information, hate speech, and offensive language highlights the more sinister facets of language change in the digital sphere. Achieving a balance between supporting language diversity, free expression, and responsible communication while reducing the negative consequences of linguistic misuse is a challenge that needs to be overcome.

Digitalizing language on social media has implications for language preservation and documentation. While social media platforms offer a dynamic space for linguistic innovation, they also pose challenges to preserving linguistic diversity and documenting endangered languages. The dominance of significant languages on global social media platforms may contribute to the marginalization of less widely spoken languages.

In conclusion, the rise of social media has indelibly shaped the evolution of language, introducing new linguistic forms, modes of expression, and cultural dynamics. Character constraints, content virality, the visual turn of emojis and memes, and the collaborative aspect of language development are examples of how social media has revolutionized language evolution. While linguistic innovation flourishes in the digital ecosystem, navigating the challenges of linguistic homogenization, ethical considerations, and the preservation of linguistic diversity in the ever-evolving landscape of social media and language is essential.

## Impact on Traditional Communication Channels

The emergence of digital communication has brought about a significant transformation, altering conventional communication routes and transforming how information is shared, accessed, and engaged. This section examines how digital communication has affected traditional channels and how print, broadcast, advertising, and interpersonal communication have changed. The dynamic interplay between digital technologies and conventional communication channels has given rise to a complex landscape marked by challenges and opportunities.

Print media, once the primary source of news and information, has undergone significant transformations in the digital age. The rise of online news platforms, digital publications, and social media has redefined how audiences access and engage with information. The immediacy and accessibility of digital news have challenged the traditional print newspaper model, leading to a decline in circulation and revenue for many print publications. Newspapers have adjusted by creating digital counterparts, embracing multimedia formats, and utilizing internet platforms for content dissemination.

The impact on broadcast journalism is equally pronounced, with digital communication influencing both the production and consumption of news. Online streaming services, podcast platforms, and social media have expanded how audiences access audio and video content. The 24-hour news cycle, fueled by digital platforms, has accelerated the pace of news dissemination, challenging traditional broadcast outlets to keep up. The democratization of information on digital media has empowered citizen journalists, bloggers, and independent content creators, reshaping the dynamics of news production and consumption.

Advertising, a cornerstone of traditional media revenue, has experienced a seismic shift in the digital era. The rise of online advertising, targeted marketing, and social media promotions has disrupted the traditional advertising model. Digital platforms allow advertisers to target particular demographics, monitor user activity, and assess campaign efficacy instantly. The shift from print and broadcast advertising to digital channels has prompted advertisers to rethink their strategies, emphasizing online presence, social media engagement, and influencer collaborations.

The impact of digital communication on interpersonal communication is most evident in social interactions and community engagement. Social media platforms are essential to people's sharing, connecting, and communication. The immediacy of messaging apps, the visual richness of multimedia content, and the global reach of social networks have redefined the parameters of interpersonal communication. However, this change is not without difficulties, as worries about online abuse, privacy, and the integrity of digital interactions surface.

The transformation of traditional communication channels by digital technologies is a multifaceted phenomenon with far-reaching implications for society. The democratization of information, the rise of user-generated content, and the decentralization of media production challenge established power structures, fostering a more participatory and diverse media landscape. But this democratization also raises questions about information accuracy, the dissemination of false information, and the possibility of echo chambers—places where people are only exposed to material that confirms their preexisting opinions.

The decline of traditional print media is a poignant illustration of the impact of digital communication. Once the primary news source for communities, newspapers faced a formidable challenge as digital platforms emerged. The immediacy, accessibility, and interactive features of online news sources have shifted readership habits, leading to a decline in newspaper circulation and advertising revenue. Print media have struggled to stay afloat in the face of shifting reader preferences, so they have had to build online paywalls, adapt to digital formats, and look into other sources of income.

Broadcast journalism, particularly television news, has undergone a metamorphosis in the digital age. The rise of online streaming services, video-sharing platforms, and podcasting has expanded how audiences consume audiovisual content. On-demand access has replaced the conventional appointment-viewing model, undermining television's position as the primary news source. News organizations have responded by developing digital platforms, engaging with audiences on social media, and experimenting with new formats to stay relevant in an evolving media landscape.

Advertising, a linchpin of traditional media revenue, has experienced a paradigm shift due to the proliferation of digital channels. Online advertising platforms, social media promotions, and influencer marketing have gained prominence, offering advertisers more targeted and measurable strategies. The traditional model of broadcast and print advertising, with its reliance on broad demographics and estimated reach, is being supplanted by data-driven digital advertising that allows for precise audience targeting and real-time analytics. Today's marketers operate in a world where social media interaction, internet visibility, and algorithmic placements are essential to the success of their campaigns.

Digital communication has a subtle yet profound effect on interpersonal communication. Social media platforms have taken center stage in people's daily lives regarding connections, communication, and sharing. The immediacy of messaging apps, the visual storytelling on platforms like Instagram, and the real-time interaction on Twitter have redefined the nature of interpersonal relationships. However, concerns about the quality of digital interactions, the potential for misinformation, and issues related to privacy and data security raise complex questions about the role of digital communication in shaping human connections.

The democratization of information is a hallmark of the digital age, challenging traditional hierarchies in media production and consumption. User-generated content, citizen journalism, and the ease of publishing on digital platforms empower individuals to participate in creating and disseminating information. This shift toward a more participatory media landscape has profound implications for the diversity of voices, the incorporation of perspectives from underrepresented groups, and the possibility for grassroots movements to gain visibility.

However, the flip side of democratization is the challenge of information quality and integrity. The ease with which information spreads on digital platforms, coupled with the potential for misinformation and disinformation, raises concerns about the reliability of content. The phenomenon of fake news, the spread of conspiracy theories, and the manipulation of online discourse for political or commercial purposes underscore the need for critical media literacy and responsible digital citizenship.

The rise of independent content creators, bloggers, and influencers exemplifies the decentralization of media production and distribution. Digital platforms allow individuals to reach global audiences without the need for traditional gatekeepers. This decentralization of influence puts classic media personalities to the test and creates new opportunities for producing niche content. However, it also introduces questions about the credibility of information, the ethics of sponsored content, and the influence of algorithmic recommendations on content consumption.

The transformation of traditional communication channels by digital technologies is not solely about displacement but also about adaptation and convergence. Recognizing the shifting landscape, traditional media outlets have embraced digital platforms to extend their reach. Newspapers have established online editions, television networks offer streaming services, and radio stations engage with audiences through podcasts. The merging of traditional and digital formats reflects a changing media landscape in which creativity and flexibility are critical to existence.

The impact on advertising extends beyond the channel shift to encompass the nature of promotional strategies. Digital advertising platforms provide an alternative to traditional broadcast and print advertising because they focus on data analytics, interactive content, and customized marketing. Advertisers can tailor messages based on user behavior, demographics, and preferences. Although this focused strategy makes ads more effective, it also brings up moral concerns about permission, privacy, and the possibility of algorithmic prejudice.

The relationship between digital and traditional communication channels is not purely one of displacement but also symbiosis. Social media complements conventional media, amplifying content, providing a space for audience engagement, and serving as a source for news discovery. News organizations use social media to disseminate breaking news, promote articles, and interact with their audience. The dynamic character of media ecosystems, where traditional and digital channels coexist and enhance one another, is reflected in this interwoven interaction.

As traditional communication channels adapt to the digital landscape, there are implications for media consumption habits and the role of gatekeepers. The standard gatekeeping function, where editors, producers, and curators determine the content that reaches the audience, has evolved in the digital era. Algorithmic curation on social media, personalized news feeds, and content recommendation algorithms shape the information individuals encounter. This shift introduces questions about algorithmic transparency, filter bubbles, and the potential for individuals to be confined to information echo chambers.

The dual nature of digital platforms characterizes the impact on interpersonal communication as both facilitators and disruptors of human connection. Social media, while providing avenues for connection and community building, also introduces challenges related to digital etiquette, online harassment, and distorted personal narratives. The carefully managed Social media profiles and the need to present an idealized vision of oneself all play a part in creating a complex dynamic in which digital connections and the subtleties of in-person contact coexist.

To sum up, the influence of digital communication over conventional channels is a complex phenomenon that affects advertising, media, and interpersonal relationships. Print media, broadcast journalism, advertising, and interpersonal communication are all changing in ways indicative of the dynamic interaction between societal adaptability and technical innovation. As traditional and digital channels converge, the challenge lies in navigating the complexities of a media landscape where innovation coexists with ethical considerations and where the democratization of information opens up new possibilities and challenges for communication in the digital age.

# Chapter 3

# Natural Language Processing (NLP)

## Understanding NLP

Natural Language Processing (NLP) represents a pivotal frontier in artificial intelligence, facilitating the interaction between humans and machines through the comprehension and generation of human language. NLP's primary goal is to close the knowledge gap between humans and computers by enabling the latter to comprehend, interpret, and react to human language in a manner that resembles that of humans. This section delves into the foundations of NLP, its key components, applications across various domains, and the challenges that persist in achieving a genuinely nuanced and context-aware language understanding.

The essence of NLP lies in its ability to equip machines with the capability to comprehend and generate human language. This involves a multifaceted approach incorporating linguistic, statistical, and computational methodologies. NLP begins with extracting relevant information from unprocessed speech or text data. This process, known as natural language understanding (NLU), encompasses syntactic analysis, semantic interpretation, and pragmatic considerations. The syntactic analysis involves parsing the grammatical structure of sentences, while semantic interpretation delves into the meaning of words and their relationships. The context in which language is employed, including subtleties like tone, intent, and cultural allusions, is covered by pragmatic considerations.

One of the fundamental challenges in NLP is the ambiguity inherent in natural language. Words often carry multiple meanings, and the interpretation of a sentence can vary based on context. Resolving this ambiguity requires advanced techniques in machine learning, where algorithms are trained on vast datasets to discern patterns, context, and semantic relationships. Named Entity Recognition (NER) is a crucial aspect of NLU, enabling systems to identify and categorize entities such as names, locations, and dates within a text. Sentiment analysis further adds a layer of complexity as machines strive to comprehend the emotional tone and subjective nuances embedded in human expression.

One example of the advancements in NLP is machine translation. A capability that automatically translates text from one language to another has transcended linguistic barriers, fostering global communication and collaboration. Early machine translation systems relied heavily on rule-based approaches, where Manual labor was required to create language rules. To transform text from one language to another. However, the advent of statistical methods and, more recently, neural networks have significantly improved the accuracy and fluency of machine translation. Systems like Google Translate employ sophisticated neural models trained on extensive bilingual corpora, enabling them to capture intricate linguistic patterns and idiosyncrasies.

Beyond translation, NLP plays a pivotal role in information retrieval and extraction. Search engines, a ubiquitous facet of the digital landscape, leverage NLP algorithms to understand user queries, interpret webpage content, and deliver relevant results. The shift in search from keyword-based to more semantic and context-aware is evidence of how NLP develops. By incorporating natural language understanding and machine learning techniques, search engines can infer user intent, understand the meaning behind queries, and provide more accurate and contextually relevant results.

The development of voice-activated virtual assistants is a prime example of how NLP is used in real-world situations. Systems like Apple's Siri, Amazon's Alexa, and Google Assistant respond to voice commands, engage in natural language conversations, and perform tasks ranging from setting reminders to providing weather updates. These virtual assistants rely on sophisticated speech recognition and NLP algorithms to decipher spoken language, infer user intent, and generate appropriate responses. This has made the interaction between humans and machines more user-friendly and accessible.

Sentiment analysis, a subfield of NLP, has gained prominence in the era of social media and online reviews. Analyzing the sentiment expressed in user-generated content allows businesses and organizations to gauge public opinion, understand customer feedback, and make data-driven decisions. Whether monitoring brand sentiment on social media or assessing product reviews, sentiment analysis algorithms process text to determine the emotional tone, sentiment polarity, and overall subjective context. Thanks to this insightful information, businesses may improve client experiences, adjust marketing strategies, and proactively handle problems.

While NLP has made remarkable strides, challenges persist in achieving a deep and nuanced understanding of human language. The linguistic diversity and heterogeneity, which includes dialects, slang, and cultural quirks, is a significant obstacle. Developing NLP models that can generalize across diverse linguistic expressions remains an ongoing area of research. Furthermore, the ambiguity included in language makes it difficult for machines to interpret metaphors, sarcasm, and context correctly. For NLP systems, these subtleties in language, which come naturally to humans, pose complex challenges.

The dynamic character of language evolution adds another layer of complexity to NLP efforts. Language is a dynamic system prone to alterations, fads, and novel manifestations. Maintaining current and flexible NLP models to accommodate new linguistic patterns is an ongoing task. Slang, neologisms, and shifts in language conventions necessitate continuous training and refinement of NLP algorithms to ensure relevance and accuracy. Furthermore, the contextual richness of language, with its dependence on shared knowledge and cultural references, poses challenges for machines in grasping the full depth and subtlety of human communication.

Ethical considerations loom large in the landscape of NLP, particularly concerning biases embedded in training data and algorithmic decision-making. NLP models are trained on vast datasets that may inadvertently encode biases present in the data, reflecting historical inequalities and societal prejudices. These biases can manifest in discriminatory outcomes, reinforcing existing disparities if not addressed vigilantly. The quest for fairness and ethical AI in NLP involves refining algorithms to mitigate biases and promoting transparency, accountability, and inclusivity in the development and deployment of NLP systems.

When cutting-edge technology is integrated, NLP's future presents many intriguing possibilities. Transfer learning, a paradigm involving pre-training models regarding massive datasets and fine-tuning them for specific purposes, has shown promise in enhancing NLP capabilities. Models like OpenAI's GPT (Generative Pre-trained Transformer) demonstrate the potential of transfer learning by achieving impressive results in language understanding and generation. This approach enables models to leverage knowledge gained from a single activity or sector to enhance performance in related areas, a step toward more generalized and adaptive language models.

The convergence of natural language processing (NLP) with other artificial intelligence (AI) fields, such as computer vision and robotics, opens the door to multimodal AI systems that can understand and engage with the world holistically. By combining language comprehension with visual and tactile inputs, machines may comprehend intricate situations, deduce users' intents, and react appropriately within the context. This synergy holds immense potential in applications ranging from assistive technologies for people with disabilities to autonomous systems that can navigate and comprehend diverse environments.

Conversational AI represents a frontier where NLP endeavors to create more natural, context-aware, and interactive dialogue systems. Progress in this domain involves improving language generation and imbuing machines with a deeper understanding of user context, emotional cues, and conversational dynamics. Virtual assistants that can engage in more human-like conversations, understand user preferences over time, and provide personalized interactions indicate the strides in enhancing conversational AI.

In conclusion, NLP stands at the forefront of AI innovation, unraveling the complexities of human language and transforming the dynamics of human-machine interaction. NLP has influenced many aspects of our digital life, including sentiment analysis, virtual assistants, machine translation, and more. Notwithstanding noteworthy advancements, difficulties continue, compelling the AI community to address linguistic diversity, moral issues, and the changing character of human communication. As NLP continues to evolve, its impact on technology, society, and how we communicate is poised to deepen, offering a glimpse into a future where machines comprehend and converse with humans in a manner that mirrors the richness and nuance of natural language.

## Applications in Everyday Life

Technology integration into our daily lives has ushered in myriad applications that permeate various aspects of our routine, enhancing efficiency, connectivity, and convenience. From the moment we wake up to the time we retire for the night, technology-driven applications significantly contribute to the formation of our experiences. This secton delves into the diverse applications that have become ubiquitous in everyday life, spanning communication, health, education, transportation, and leisure, illustrating technology's profound impact on our daily routines.

Among the many uses of technology in our daily lives, communication stands out as being particularly prevalent. The advent of smartphones and messaging applications has transformed how we connect and interact with others. Platforms like WhatsApp, Facebook Messenger, and iMessage facilitate instant communication, breaking geographical barriers and enabling real-time conversations. Social media applications like Instagram, Twitter, and TikTok provide platforms for sharing experiences, opinions, and creative expressions, fostering a digital ecosystem where individuals connect, communicate, and build communities.

The realm of health has witnessed a revolution with the advent of health and fitness applications. Applications such as Fitbit, MyFitnessPal, and Apple Health enable people to measure their physical activity, nutrition, and general health through devices like step counts and calorie counters. These applications provide personalized insights, goal tracking, and motivational features, encouraging users to adopt healthier lifestyles. Telemedicine applications allow remote consultations with healthcare professionals, enhancing accessibility and convenience in seeking medical advice.

Education has undergone a transformative shift with the proliferation of e-learning applications. Access to abundant educational resources, courses, and tutorials is made possible by platforms such as Khan Academy, Coursera, and Duolingo. These applications cater to diverse learning styles, allowing users to acquire new skills, pursue academic interests, or engage in professional development from the comfort of their homes. Integrating virtual classrooms, interactive quizzes, and collaborative tools has reshaped the education landscape, making learning more accessible and flexible.

Applications that improve travel experiences and expedite commute have changed transportation. Uber and Lyft are two ride-sharing businesses that have revolutionized how people travel around cities by providing alternatives to traditional taxis that are both more economical and more convenient. Provide real-time traffic information, optimal routes, and turn-by-turn directions, simplifying navigation and reducing travel time. Electric scooter and bike-sharing applications contribute to sustainable urban mobility, offering on-demand transportation options.

Financial management has become more accessible and efficient with the advent of banking and finance applications. Mobile banking apps enable users to check balances, transfer funds, and manage transactions from their smartphones. Budgeting applications like Mint and YNAB assist individuals in tracking expenses, setting financial goals, and optimizing their financial health. Investment platforms provide users with tools to monitor portfolios, analyze market trends, and make informed investment decisions, democratizing access to financial markets.

The influence of technology extends into the domain of leisure and entertainment, enriching our recreational experiences. Streaming services like Netflix, Spotify, and YouTube offer on-demand access to various movies, music, and videos, revolutionizing how we consume content. Diverse gaming interests are catered to via gaming programs on cellphones, consoles, and PCs, which promote immersive and engaging experiences. Examples of applications that utilize augmented reality (AR) and virtual reality (VR) introduce new dimensions to entertainment, allowing users to engage with content in innovative and immersive ways.

Smart home applications have transformed how we interact with our living spaces, introducing automation and connectivity to everyday appliances. Home automation systems like Amazon Alexa and Google Home enable voice-controlled interactions with lights, thermostats, and smart devices. Security applications with remote monitoring and surveillance features provide homeowners peace of mind and enhanced control over their living environments. Smart home appliances like thermostats and refrigerators are included to create linked and effective living environments.

The workforce has experienced a paradigm shift with the widespread adoption of productivity applications. Tools like Microsoft Office, Google Workspace, and Slack facilitate collaboration, document sharing, and communication in professional settings. Project management applications like Trello and Asana streamline task organization, project tracking, and team coordination. Video conferencing applications, like Zoom and Microsoft Teams, are now essential to remote work since they allow for virtual meetings, presentations, and cross-border cooperation.

With the introduction of applications for local services, restaurants, and transportation, navigating urban surroundings has gotten easier. Users can arrange rides, supervise drivers, and make payments using their mobile devices through ride-sharing services such as Uber and Lyft. These services provide a convenient alternative to traditional taxis. Apps that transport food, like DoorDash and Uber Eats, change how people eat by bringing a wide variety of gourmet options to their door. Local service applications like Yelp and TripAdvisor provide reviews, recommendations, and information about businesses, attractions, and events in specific locations.

Applications designed to streamline tasks and boost productivity have enhanced personal organization and time management. Calendar applications like Google Calendar and Apple Calendar assist users in scheduling events, setting reminders, and managing appointments. To-do list applications such as Todoist and Wunderlist enable users to organize tasks, prioritize activities, and track progress. Note-taking applications like Evernote and Microsoft OneNote facilitate the capture and organization of ideas, thoughts, and information, serving as digital notebooks.

Applications that transform cell phones into potent cameras and editing tools have changed the realm of photography. Camera applications with advanced features and manual controls allow users to capture high-quality photos. Photo editing applications like Adobe Lightroom and Snapseed offer many tools for enhancing and manipulating images, allowing users to unleash their creative expressions. Incorporating photo-sharing tools into social media platforms such as Instagram and Snapchat helps cultivate communities that involve creative expression and visual storytelling.

Socialization as a field has developed with apps that help organize meetings, get-togethers, and shared experiences. Users can connect with friends, exchange updates, and interact with material on social networking apps like Facebook, Instagram, and Twitter. Tinder and Bumble, among other dating apps, have entirely changed how people meet possible mates and the dynamics of romantic relationships. Event applications like Meetup and Eventbrite enable users to discover and participate in various activities, from social gatherings to cultural events.

Applications for accessibility have become ground-breaking instruments for guaranteeing inclusivity and equitable access to data and services. Screen reader applications assist individuals with visual impairments in accessing digital content through voice synthesis. Speech-to-text applications provide a voice for individuals with speech disabilities, enabling them to communicate effectively. Captioning applications enhance the accessibility of video content for individuals with hearing impairments, promoting inclusivity in the digital realm.

Even while the abundance of applications has unquestionably changed how we live our daily lives, specific issues must be acknowledged and resolved. Strong security measures and open procedures are essential for creating and implementing applications because they address privacy issues, data security, and the moral ramifications of data collection. Achieving an equilibrium between inventiveness and conscientious application is essential for fully utilizing technology in our everyday lives.

In conclusion, the applications that have become integral to everyday life span a diverse spectrum, impacting how we communicate, work, learn, travel, and entertain ourselves. The smooth incorporation of technology into our daily lives has improved productivity, reach, and accessibility in several areas. The landscape of applications will surely change much more as technology advances, influencing how we navigate and perceive the world in the years to come.

## NLP's Role in Information Retrieval

Natural Language Processing (NLP) serves as a cornerstone in information retrieval, revolutionizing how we access and interact with vast amounts of textual data. At its core, NLP strives to bridge the gap between human language and computer understanding, enabling machines to comprehend, interpret, and respond to natural language queries. Information retrieval, a critical component of our digital landscape, involves extracting relevant information from massive datasets. NLP's role in this process is multifaceted, encompassing tasks such as text processing, semantic analysis, and language understanding, all aimed at enhancing the accuracy and efficiency of retrieving pertinent information.

NLP's fundamental capability in information retrieval is its comprehension and processing of human language. Conventional information retrieval systems focused on keyword-based queries, frequently producing results that were too general or irrelevant to the context. NLP introduces a nuanced understanding of language, allowing systems to interpret the meaning behind queries and consider the context in which specific terms are used. This semantic richness enables more precise and context-aware information retrieval, aligning results closely with the user's intent.

Semantic search is a paradigm that aims to improve user queries and document content interpretation through natural language processing (NLP). Semantic search engines, such as Google's BERT (Bidirectional Encoder Representations from Transformers), leverage advanced NLP methods for analyzing the context of a question and the relationships between the terms in the query. This allows the algorithm to interpret unclear phrases and provide more precise search results. Semantic search improves the relevance of retrieved information and contributes to a more natural and conversational interaction between users and search engines.

In the context of information retrieval, document summarization is a crucial NLP task that aids in presenting concise and informative snippets of content. Autonomous summarization algorithms, frequently driven by natural language processing (NLP) models, examine documents and extract significant details, enabling users to understand the main ideas of a text without reading it cover to cover. This is particularly valuable when users need quick insights or when dealing with extensive textual data. NLP-driven summarization techniques contribute to more efficient information retrieval by presenting users with condensed yet meaningful representations of documents.

Another aspect of natural language processing (NLP) essential to information retrieval is named entity recognition (NER). NER involves identifying and classifying entities within a given text, such as names of people, organizations, locations, dates, and more. Integrating NER into information retrieval processes enhances extracting specific and relevant information from documents. For example, in a news article, NER can identify and categorize the names of individuals, locations, and organizations mentioned, providing users with structured and easily navigable information.

One notable development in NLP's contribution to information retrieval is the creation of question-answering systems. Models for answering questions, such as those built on transformer architectures, are intended to comprehend user inquiries and provide conversational responses. These models make use of contextual data to produce precise and pertinent answers. This capability is precious in information retrieval scenarios where users seek specific information or have nuanced queries. Integrating question-answering systems enhances the precision and user-friendliness of information retrieval interfaces.

Sentiment analysis, a subfield of NLP, also plays a role in information retrieval, especially in user-generated content. Analyzing the sentiment expressed in reviews, comments, or social media posts contributes to a more nuanced understanding of retrieved information. For instance, sentiment analysis can discern whether a product review is positive or negative, providing users with additional insights beyond factual information. This emotional layer enhances the relevance and user experience in information retrieval, particularly in scenarios where user opinions and sentiments are integral to decision-making.

Machine translation is a classic NLP application that affects information retrieval in multilingual environments. In a globalized digital landscape, where information is available in multiple languages, machine translation systems enable users to retrieve and comprehend content in their preferred language. NLP-driven translation models, such as those employing neural machine translation, not only facilitate language accessibility but also contribute to cross-cultural information retrieval. Users can explore and understand content from diverse linguistic sources, broadening the scope of information retrieval on a global scale.

The evolution of information retrieval systems has witnessed the integration of conversational agents and virtual assistants powered by NLP. These systems, such as chatbots or voice-activated assistants, engage in natural conversations with users, understand queries, and provide relevant information. NLP-driven conversational agents offer a more intuitive and user-friendly information retrieval experience, especially when users prefer interactive and dialog-based interactions.

The advent of pre-trained language models, exemplified by OpenAI's GPT (Generative Pre-trained Transformer) series, has significantly impacted information retrieval capabilities. These models get a profound comprehension of semantics, context, and linguistic subtleties through extensive training on a wide range of text data. Optimized for specific information retrieval tasks, these models show improved comprehension of user requests and produce appropriate responses for the given context. The versatility of pre-trained language models extends to various domains, making them valuable assets in refining and optimizing information retrieval systems.

Even with NLP's incredible advancements in information retrieval, there are always problems that need to be solved, necessitating continued study and creativity. The variety and fluctuation of language, which includes slang, colloquialisms, and cultural quirks, is a significant obstacle. NLP models must navigate this linguistic complexity to ensure accurate interpretation and retrieval of information. The challenge of handling ambiguous queries, where user intent may not be explicitly clear, remains a focal point for improvement in information retrieval systems. Furthermore, significant thought should be given to the ethical issues of bias in language models and potential discrepancies in information retrieval results.

NLP's trajectory in information retrieval has a lot of exciting things in store, thanks to both changing user needs and technological developments. Continued research in explainable AI, where models provide transparent insights into decision-making processes, can enhance user trust and understanding of information retrieval systems. The exploration of multimodal approaches, combining text with other modalities such as images or audio, presents opportunities for more comprehensive and context-aware information retrieval. Furthermore, integrating domain-specific knowledge and ontologies can refine information retrieval in specialized fields, tailoring results to specific user requirements.

In conclusion, NLP's role in information retrieval is transformative, reshaping how we access, understand, and interact with textual information. NLP techniques contribute to a more nuanced, efficient, and user-centric information retrieval experience, from semantic search and document summarization to named entity recognition and question-answering. As technology advances, the synergy between NLP and information retrieval holds the promise of further innovations, enriching how we navigate the vast landscape of digital information.

# Chapter 4

# AI and Language

**Conversational AI**

Conversational Artificial Intelligence (AI) represents a paradigm shift in human-computer interaction, ushering in a new era where machines engage in natural language conversations with users. At its core, conversational AI aims to bridge the gap between humans and machines, enabling intuitive, context-aware, and interactive dialogues. This section investigates the origins, uses, difficulties, and prospects for conversational AI, focusing on its revolutionary effects on several facets of our digital environment.

Neural Language Processing (NLP), a subfield of artificial intelligence that focuses on giving robots the ability to comprehend, interpret, and produce human language, is the cornerstone of conversational AI. NLP algorithms process linguistic input, discerning meanings, context, and nuances to facilitate communication. The advent of advanced NLP models, often powered by deep learning architectures like transformers, has significantly elevated the capabilities of conversational AI. These models can comprehend intricate linguistic patterns, discern users' intentions, and provide responses that resemble real-world human dialogue.

Conversational AI finds applications across various domains, reshaping how we interact with technology daily. Virtual assistants, such as Apple's Siri, Amazon's Alexa, and Google Assistant, exemplify the integration of conversational AI into everyday scenarios. Users can issue voice commands, ask questions, and receive responses conversationally, creating a more natural and user-friendly interaction. These virtual assistants employ natural language processing (NLP) models to comprehend customer inquiries, collect pertinent data, and carry out activities, from sending out reminders to giving weather updates.

Customer service has been transformed by incorporating conversational AI in chatbots and virtual agents. Businesses use chatbots on their websites and messaging apps to interact with clients in real-time, providing support, responding to questions, and easing purchases. The ability of conversational AI to provide instant responses, operate 24/7, and handle multiple interactions simultaneously enhances customer support efficiency. Additionally, sentiment analysis capabilities enable chatbots to gauge user emotions and tailor responses accordingly, contributing to a more personalized customer experience.

With its ability to provide dynamic and flexible learning environments, conversational AI is vital to education. Chatbots designed for educational purposes can assist students in understanding concepts, answering queries, and providing additional resources. These conversational agents leverage NLP to comprehend user inputs, adapting their responses based on individual learning styles and progress. The interactive nature of conversational AI in education fosters engagement, supports personalized learning paths, and complements traditional teaching methods.

In healthcare, conversational AI applications extend to virtual health assistants and chatbots that assist users with medical information, appointment scheduling, and symptom analysis. Conversational agents can engage in dialogues with users to gather relevant health information, provide preliminary assessments, and offer guidance on seeking medical attention. Conversational AI facilitates smooth interactions that improve access to healthcare information, particularly when users need fast and dependable support.

The e-commerce sector has embraced conversational AI to enhance the online shopping experience. NLP-powered virtual shopping assistants can recognize customer preferences, make product recommendations, and assist consumers with buying. About e-commerce platforms, conversational assistants can respond to product questions, offer sales details, and make order tracking easier. The conversational interface mimics the help one could get in a physical store, making online buying more individualized and user-centric.

Conversational AI has many uses, but drawbacks also need to be carefully considered and researched further. One significant challenge is the need for systems to comprehend user intent accurately. Because of the inherent complexities present in spoken language, users can convey their meaning in various ways. Language variability, such as slang, colloquialisms, and cultural quirks, makes it difficult for conversational AI models to understand user inputs correctly. The quest for more sophisticated intent recognition mechanisms remains a focus area to enhance the precision of casual AI systems.

Context awareness is another crucial aspect that poses challenges in conversational AI. Human conversations often rely on contextual cues, references to prior statements, and shared knowledge. It isn't easy to create AI systems that can retain and use context during several turns in a discussion. Context-aware conversational AI models must comprehend both the immediate user input and the larger context of the continuing debate. Achieving a deeper level of context awareness is essential for systems to generate coherent and relevant responses, fostering more natural and engaging interactions.

The ethical dimensions of conversational AI introduce considerations related to user privacy, data security, and potential biases in language models. Casual AI systems often rely on vast datasets for training, and these datasets may inadvertently encode biases present in the data. Biases can manifest in responses that reflect societal prejudices, reinforcing stereotypes or discriminatory perspectives. Ethical AI practices involve ongoing efforts to mitigate biases, ensure transparency in conversational AI decision-making, and prioritize user privacy in the collection and storage of conversational data.

User trust is a critical factor in the adoption and success of conversational AI. Consumers must believe that their communications with conversational agents are safe, confidential, and devoid of false information. In addition to resolving technological issues, establishing trust requires transparency about casual AI systems' strengths and weaknesses. Ensuring that users understand when interacting with an AI system, providing options for human escalation in critical scenarios, and incorporating user feedback in model refinement contribute to fostering trust in conversational AI.

The future trajectory of conversational AI holds exciting possibilities, driven by ongoing advancements in AI research and technology. Multimodal conversational AI, which integrates text and visual and auditory inputs, presents avenues for more immersive and comprehensive interactions. Integrating emotional intelligence into conversational AI involves recognizing and responding to user emotions, contributing to more empathetic and human-like interactions. Continued research in reinforcement learning and unsupervised learning aims to enhance conversational AI's ability to learn and adapt over time, refining responses based on user feedback and evolving language patterns.

**Language Models and Their Impacts**

Advanced artificial intelligence (AI) architectures have enabled language models, in particular, to become revolutionary technologies, reshaping many aspects of our digital environment. These models, designed to understand, generate, and manipulate human language, have far-reaching impacts on diverse fields, from natural language processing and content generation to human-computer interaction and information retrieval. This essay delves into the theoretical underpinnings, practical uses, moral dilemmas, and prospective directions of language models, illuminating their significant impact on human communication, content creation, and technological interaction.

The foundations of modern language models rest on natural language processing (NLP), a subdomain of AI dedicated to enabling machines to understand and process human language. Traditional rule-based approaches were superseded by statistical methods and, more recently, by deep learning techniques that leverage neural networks. The advent of transformer architectures, such as OpenAI's GPT (Generative Pre-trained Transformer) series, has propelled language models to new heights of sophistication. These models get an intricate knowledge of linguistic nuances, syntactic structures, and semantic linkages through pre-training on large volumes of heterogeneous text material.

Language models have many uses and are altering information creation and our interactions with technology. In natural language processing, these models are the backbone for sentiment analysis, named entity recognition, and machine translation tasks. Sentiment analysis algorithms leverage language models to discern the emotional tone and subjective nuances embedded in textual content, providing valuable insights into public opinion, customer feedback, and social trends. Recognizing and categorizing various kinds of entities is referred to as named entity recognition (NER). Examples include names, locations, and organizations within a text, making it easier to extract and organize information.

One of the most impactful applications of language models is in the realm of content generation. Text completion, summarization, and creative writing are areas where language models showcase their versatility. Auto-completion features in search engines and messaging applications leverage language models to predict and suggest the following words or phrases as users type. Document summarization algorithms, powered by these models, provide concise yet informative summaries of lengthy texts, streamlining information retrieval and consumption. The creative potential of language models is exemplified by their ability to generate coherent and contextually relevant text based on given prompts.

Machine translation, a longstanding challenge in NLP, has witnessed significant advancements with the application of language models. Neural machine translation models, incorporating transformer architectures, excel in capturing intricate linguistic patterns and nuances, leading to more accurate and fluent translations. Platforms like Google Translate leverage these models to provide near-instant translations across many languages, fostering global communication and collaboration.

The impact of language models extends to human-computer interaction, particularly in the development of virtual assistants and chatbots. Language models employ virtual assistants such as Siri, Alexa, and Google Assistant to comprehend the inquiries made by users, determine their level of intent, and produce suitable responses.

Chatbots, deployed on websites and messaging platforms, engage in natural language conversations with users, providing assistance, answering queries, and facilitating transactions. By incorporating language models, these interactive systems become more natural and easier to use, making distinguishing between human and computer communication harder.

Language models are essential for improving search engine skills in information retrieval. For instance, Google's BERT (Bidirectional Encoder Representations from Transformers) understands the context and relationships between words in a search query, leading to more accurate and context-aware search results. The application of language models in information retrieval extends to question-answering systems, where models are trained to comprehend and respond to user queries in a manner that mimics human understanding.

Even with the notable developments and uses, the emergence of language models raises ethical questions that must be carefully considered. The possibility that biases incorporated in the training data will show up in language models is one major worry. Models trained on large and diverse datasets may inadvertently learn and perpetuate biases present in the data, reflecting historical inequalities, stereotypes, or societal prejudices. Addressing discrimination in language models involves refining algorithms to mitigate biases, implementing strategies for ethical data collection, and curating diverse training datasets.

The ethical use of language models extends to concerns about misinformation, disinformation, and the generation of inappropriate or harmful content. If not adequately supervised or fine-tuned, language models can generate text that may be misleading, offensive, or violate ethical standards. The responsibility lies not only with developers and researchers but also with the platforms and organizations deploying these models to implement safeguards, moderation mechanisms, and content filters to ensure responsible and ethical use.

Privacy considerations also emerge as language models become more sophisticated in understanding and generating human-like text. The fine line between personalization and intrusion raises questions about data security, consent, and the potential for language models to process and store sensitive information. Robust privacy policies, open practices, and easily navigable controls over data sharing and storage are necessary to provide tailored experiences while maintaining user privacy.

The future trajectories of language models involve advancements that address these ethical considerations and push the boundaries of their capabilities. Explainability in AI, particularly in language models, garners significant attention. Creating models that offer clear insights into their decision-making procedures improves user comprehension and confidence. Explainable AI not only aids in addressing biases but also empowers users to comprehend how language models arrive at specific conclusions or generate particular responses.

Continued research toward democratizing access to language models represents a promising avenue. OpenAI's initiatives, such as GPT-3's availability through APIs, mark a step towards making advanced language models more accessible to developers and businesses. This democratization fosters innovation and diverse applications, from content creation and natural language interfaces to personalized user experiences.

Multimodal language models, capable of understanding and generating text and other modalities such as images and audio, represent the next frontier. Integrating visual and auditory inputs into language models enables a more comprehensive understanding of content, opening avenues for applications in areas like image captioning, content moderation, and accessibility for individuals with visual or auditory impairments.

The intersection of language models with reinforcement learning holds the potential to create models that can adapt and learn from user feedback over time. Language models can be improved by applying reinforcement learning frameworks, which consider user interactions, changing linguistic patterns, and dynamic situations. Language models become more relevant and context-aware due to their adaptability, improving their sensitivity to user preferences and communication styles.

Emotional intelligence is an emerging dimension in the development of language models. Models that understand and respond to user emotions contribute to more empathetic and human-like interactions. Emotional intelligence in language models involves recognizing and appropriately responding to emotional cues expressed in text, creating a more nuanced and responsive user experience.

In summary, language models powered by cutting-edge AI architectures are revolutionizing how humans engage with technology and create content. From natural language processing tasks to content generation, these models exhibit versatility and transformative potential. But as they become more popular, moral questions arise that need careful design, implementation, and use. As language models evolve, their impact on communication, creativity, and human-computer interaction is poised to deepen. It offers a glimpse into a future where machines and humans engage in increasingly sophisticated and meaningful linguistic exchanges.

## AI and Personalized Communication

Artificial Intelligence (AI) has ushered in personalized communication at the beginning of this new era, fundamentally transforming how individuals interact with digital technologies. The integration of AI-driven personalized communication is evident across various platforms, from social media and e-commerce to virtual assistants and email services. This section explores AI's foundations, applications, challenges, and future trajectories in personalized communication, shedding light on its implications for user experiences, marketing strategies, and the evolving landscape of human-machine interactions.

At the heart of AI's impact on personalized communication lies the ability of machine learning algorithms to analyze vast datasets and discern patterns, preferences, and behaviors. The foundations of personalized touch are rooted in tailoring information and interactions to individual users based on their unique characteristics, preferences, and historical interactions. Dynamic and adaptive communication tactics that employ AI to give content, recommendations, and interactions catered to each user's unique needs and interests are replacing traditional one-size-fits-all approaches.

Social media platforms are prime examples of AI's ubiquitous impact on tailored communication. Algorithms embedded in platforms like Facebook, Instagram, and Twitter analyze user behavior, engagement patterns, and content preferences to curate personalized feeds. The content displayed to users is not merely chronological but is algorithmically tailored, considering factors such as user interactions, content relevance, and previous engagement. This personalized approach enhances user satisfaction and retention, creating an experience where individuals are more likely to encounter content aligned with their interests.

The application of AI-driven tailored communication has revolutionized e-commerce. Using machine learning algorithms, recommendation engines examine users' browsing habits, past purchases, and interests to make personalized recommendations for goods and services. Platforms like Amazon and Netflix leverage these recommendation algorithms to give users a curated selection of items or content, fostering a more engaging and personalized shopping or entertainment experience. Not only do customized product recommendations improve user satisfaction, but they also boost sales and foster client loyalty.

Virtual assistants, such as Apple's Siri, Amazon's Alexa, and Google Assistant, showcase the integration of AI in personalized communication through natural language processing and machine learning. These helpers comprehend user inquiries, adjust to unique speech patterns, and offer appropriate responses for the given situation. As users interact more with these virtual assistants, the systems learn and adapt, refining their understanding and answers. This iterative learning process contributes to a personalized and user-centric interaction model, creating a sense of continuity and adaptability in the virtual assistant's communication.

Email communication has evolved with the infusion of AI, enabling marketers to craft personalized and targeted campaigns. AI-powered email marketing platforms examine user behavior, engagement metrics, and past data to customize subject lines, content, and timing. Personalization in email campaigns extends beyond addressing recipients by their names; it involves delivering content that aligns with their preferences, purchase history, and interactions with previous emails. As a result, users will receive more relevant and exciting emails, increasing the chance that they will interact and convert.

Even with the numerous advantages, several obstacles must be addressed when integrating AI into personalized communication. The gathering and analyzing of user data raises concerns about data security, consent, and the appropriate use of personal information, putting privacy issues front and center. Maintaining a healthy equilibrium between providing individualized experiences and safeguarding user privacy requires transparent data policies, robust security measures, and user-friendly data sharing and storage controls.

The possibility of algorithmic bias presents another difficulty since AI models may unintentionally reinforce or magnify preexisting prejudices in the training set. Biased algorithms may produce discriminatory content recommendations, unequal access to information, or reinforcing prejudices in personalized communication. Addressing algorithmic bias involves continuous monitoring, ethical data curation, and the development of algorithms that are sensitive to and actively counteract tendencies.

The interpretability of AI models is a critical consideration in personalized communication. Users are often presented with customized content or recommendations generated by complex algorithms, and understanding how these recommendations are arrived at can be challenging. Improving the interpretability of AI models entails creating techniques that offer clear insights into decision-making procedures, guaranteeing that users can understand and rely on the customized experiences these systems provide.

Future developments in AI-powered personalized communication will focus on resolving these issues and improving user experiences. Context-aware personalization represents a promising avenue where AI systems consider individual user preferences and factor in the broader context of user interactions. Understanding the situational context allows AI systems to deliver more nuanced and relevant personalized communication that adapts to users' changing needs and circumstances.

Natural language processing and sentiment analysis advancements contribute to more emotionally intelligent AI systems. Personalized communication can benefit from AI models that understand the explicit content of user interactions and discern emotional nuances and sentiments. Emotionally intelligent AI can tailor responses, recommendations, and content in a way that resonates with users on an emotional level, fostering deeper engagement and connection.

Multimodal data integration—text, image, and audio—can improve tailored communication. AI models capable of understanding and generating content across multiple modalities enable more comprehensive and dynamic user experiences. For example, a virtual assistant could provide personalized recommendations based on text queries, analyze images, or understand voice inputs. This multidimensional approach contributes to a more immersive and contextually aware personalized communication model.

Collaborative filtering, a technique that recommends items based on similar users' preferences, continues to evolve with AI advancements. Integrating federated learning, where machine learning models are trained across decentralized devices, presents opportunities for personalized communication without centralizing user data. This approach addresses privacy concerns by keeping user data on local devices while still benefiting from the collaborative insights of a decentralized AI model.

The future of AI in personalized communication also involves more excellent user agency and control. Empowering users with more granular control over their personalization settings, preferences, and the types of data used for personalization allows individuals to shape their personalized experiences. Customizable AI interfaces and personalization dashboards can give users transparency and control, ensuring personalized communication aligns with their comfort levels and preferences.

In conclusion, AI's role in personalized communication has redefined how individuals engage with digital platforms, services, and technologies. From social media algorithms to virtual assistants and targeted marketing, AI-driven personalized communication has become integral to the user experience. Even if issues with privacy, bias, and interpretability still exist, continued research and moral considerations influence how AI is used in personalized communication. The convergence of ethical AI practices, user-centric personalization, and creative thinking will open up new possibilities for customized communication in the future, ensuring that it is intelligent and considerate of users' privacy and preferences.

# Chapter 5

# The Future of Linguistic Technology

**Emerging Technologies in Linguistics**

Emerging technologies in linguistics have ushered in a new era of exploration and understanding, transforming how we study, analyze, and interact with language. The scientific study of language and its structure is known as linguistics and contains several subfields. The science has reached new heights thanks to the introduction of cutting-edge technologies. This essay delves into several key emerging technologies in linguistics, exploring their applications, implications, and the transformative impact they bring to our understanding of language and communication.

The application of Natural Language Processing (NLP) is one of the most significant developments that has occurred in the field of linguistic research. To enable robots to understand, interpret, and produce human language, natural language processing (NLP) combines linguistics with artificial intelligence. NLP applications range from machine translation and sentiment analysis to named entity recognition and question-answering systems. Modern NLP models, such as transformers, have demonstrated remarkable capabilities in capturing contextual nuances and syntactic structures, making them invaluable tools for linguists studying the intricacies of language use in various contexts.

Machine translation, a prominent application of NLP, has witnessed significant advancements, reshaping cross-cultural communication. Technologies like neural machine translation employ deep learning architectures to enhance translation accuracy and fluency. Platforms like Google Translate leverage these technologies to provide near-instant translations across numerous languages. Machine translation facilitates communication between individuals who speak different languages and allows for studying language evolution and variation across diverse linguistic landscapes.

Another groundbreaking technology in linguistics is speech recognition. As advancements in machine learning continue, speech recognition systems have become more accurate and accessible. These systems, powered by deep neural networks, can rapidly transcribe spoken language into text. Speech recognition has applications in language documentation, aiding linguists in capturing and analyzing oral traditions, dialects, and endangered languages. Additionally, it contributes to developing voice-activated technologies, enabling natural language interactions with devices and virtual assistants.

The field of computational linguistics represents a confluence of linguistics and computer science, focusing on developing algorithms and models for linguistic analysis. Computational linguistics plays a vital role in parsing and analyzing large datasets of linguistic information. Techniques such as corpus linguistics involve the study of language through extensive collections of written or spoken texts. These corpora are essential for linguistic research because they allow studies of language usage trends, grammatical structure, and semantic changes throughout time.

Advancements in neuroimaging technologies have provided unprecedented insights into the neural basis of language processing. Functional magnetic resonance imaging, sometimes known as fMRI, indicates the MEG, which stands for magnetoencephalography, allowing researchers to observe brain activity associated with language tasks in real-time. Neuroimaging studies contribute to understanding how different brain regions are involved in language comprehension, production, and acquisition. This technology has implications for clinical linguistics, offering insights into language disorders and neuroplasticity.

Eye-tracking technology has revolutionized the study of language processing by providing detailed information about visual attention during reading or listening. Eye-tracking systems capture eye movements during written or spoken language interactions, providing researchers with valuable information on reading habits, comprehension techniques, and cognitive processes. This technology has applications in psycholinguistics, enabling investigations into the relationship between eye movements and language understanding.

Recent years have seen an increase in the incorporation of artificial intelligence (AI) in linguistics, which has extended to developing conversational agents and chatbots. These AI-driven systems use natural language conversations with users, simulating human-like interactions. Conversational agents have applications in language learning, customer support, and virtual assistance. They provide linguists a platform to research language pragmatics, the sociolinguistics of language use in digital communication, and human-machine interactions.

The linguistics field also embraces the potential of technology applications such as augmented reality (AR) and virtual reality (VR) are examples of such applications. Through immersive experiences provided by virtual reality environments, linguists can investigate language use in simulated contexts. For instance, researchers can create virtual language immersion scenarios to explore language acquisition or study linguistic behavior in controlled virtual environments. Conversely, augmented reality (AR) applications increase the physical world with digital overlays, allowing linguists to examine language inside situational contexts.

The exploration of linguistic landscapes has been revolutionized using Geographic Information Systems (GIS) technology. Using GIS, linguists can map language interaction, diversity, and characteristics at spatial scales. By overlaying linguistic data on maps, researchers gain insights into spatial patterns of language distribution, the impact of geography on language evolution, and the dynamics of language contact in multilingual regions.

In the realm of sociolinguistics, social media analysis has become a valuable tool for studying language variation, change, and sociolinguistic trends. Computational methods enable researchers to analyze large datasets of user-generated content, uncovering patterns of linguistic variation across different demographics, regions, and social groups. Social media platforms serve as linguistic laboratories, offering a dynamic and evolving dataset for studying contemporary language use.

The emergence of blockchain technology has implications for linguistic research, particularly in linguistic data management and preservation. Blockchain offers a decentralized, safe framework for linguistic dataset storage that promotes data integrity and cooperative study. Linguists can use blockchain to create transparent and immutable records of language data, addressing issues of reproducibility and data reliability in linguistic studies.

Applying biometric technologies to linguistics introduces the concept of "talker identification" or speaker recognition. Biometric voice analysis verifies and identifies people using their speech patterns. This technology has forensic applications, aiding in voice recognition for legal and security purposes. Additionally, it advances the study of voice as a distinct linguistic marker by enabling researchers to examine individual variations in speech patterns, intonation, and pronunciation.

Quantum computing, an emerging field in computing technology, holds the potential for transformative applications in linguistics. Quantum computers can perform by applying the principles of quantum mechanics—complex computations at speeds far surpassing classical computers. In linguistics, quantum computing may contribute to solving computationally intensive tasks, such as large-scale language modeling and complex linguistic simulations, at unprecedented speeds.

Despite the myriad advancements, integrating technology in linguistics comes with challenges and ethical considerations. Addressing concerns about data privacy, informed permission, and the appropriate use of linguistic data is crucial. As technology facilitates the collection of vast amounts of linguistic information, researchers must navigate ethical guidelines to protect participant privacy and adhere to principles of responsible data management.

Furthermore, concerns about the digital divide raise questions about the inclusivity of technological advancements in linguistics. Access to cutting-edge technologies may be limited in specific communities or regions, potentially leading to gaps in linguistic research representation. Researchers must be aware of these disparities and strive for inclusivity in applying technological tools in linguistic studies.

In conclusion, integrating emerging technologies in linguistics has revolutionized the field, offering new avenues for exploration and understanding. From NLP and machine translation to neuroimaging and sociolinguistic analysis of social media, these technologies provide linguists with powerful tools to delve into the complexities of language. As the technological landscape continues to evolve, linguistics positions itself at the crossroads where innovation and tradition meet to harness the potential of emerging technologies to unravel the mysteries of language and communication in unprecedented ways.

## Augmented Reality and Language

Augmented reality (AR) can completely change how we interact and perceive language in our environment. This essay explores the intersection of augmented reality and language, examining the applications, implications, and transformative impact AR brings to language learning, communication and how we engage with linguistic content in the physical world.

AR provides a dynamic and immersive learning environment, enabling learners to interact with virtual language elements overlaid with their physical surroundings. Language learners can use AR-enabled devices like smartphones or AR glasses to access digital content, translations, and language exercises seamlessly integrated into real-world contexts. For instance, learners can point their devices at objects or signs to receive instant translations, view language-related information, or engage in interactive language exercises, creating a more contextual and engaging learning experience.

The gamification of language learning through augmented reality represents a novel approach to engage learners and enhance their linguistic proficiency. AR language games use the actual world as a platform for interactive tests, challenges, and language practice. Learners can explore their surroundings, interact with virtual characters or objects, and practice language skills in a playful and immersive manner. This gamified approach makes language learning more enjoyable and fosters a sense of exploration and discovery, motivating learners to engage with the language actively in diverse contexts.

In language education, augmented reality enables the creation of interactive and customizable language materials. Educators can develop AR-enhanced textbooks, worksheets, or learning materials integrating digital content, multimedia, and interactive elements. Students can use AR devices to access additional information, videos, or interactive quizzes linked to specific lessons, enhancing their understanding and retention of linguistic concepts. Because AR information is dynamic, it may be updated and modified regularly, keeping language resources up to date and in line with changing educational requirements.

Augmented reality also contributes to cultural and linguistic immersion experiences. Language learners can use AR applications to explore virtual environments that simulate real-world cultural contexts and linguistic scenarios. For example, learners studying a foreign language can use AR to virtually visit a marketplace, engage in conversations with virtual native speakers, or participate in cultural events. This immersive approach gives learners a deeper understanding of language use in authentic situations, promoting cultural awareness and enhancing their ability to communicate effectively in diverse settings.

In addition to language learning, augmented reality has implications for multilingual communication and translation. AR devices equipped with real-time translation capabilities enable users to view translated text overlays in their field of vision. This facilitates seamless communication in multilingual environments, allowing users to understand and respond to written information or spoken language in real-time. When pointed at the written text, AR translation apps can instantly provide translations, enabling users to overcome language barriers and access information in their preferred language.

Augmented reality enhances the accessibility of language-related information in physical spaces. Museums, historical sites, and cultural landmarks can deploy AR to provide visitors with multilingual information, interactive exhibits, and virtual guides. Users can point their AR devices at shows to access additional details, historical context, or audio guides in their chosen language. This enriches the visitor experience and accommodates diverse linguistic preferences, ensuring that language does not hinder understanding and appreciating cultural heritage.

The integration of AR in language-related applications extends to professional contexts, particularly in fields that require multilingual communication. AR-enhanced meetings and conferences can provide real-time language translation overlays, allowing participants to follow discussions in their preferred language. AR's ability to enable successful communication across linguistic barriers and promote cross-cultural understanding has ramifications for international collaboration, diplomacy, and global corporate communication.

Novel approaches to storytelling and narrative experiences that combine the digital and physical worlds are brought to life by augmented reality. AR storytelling applications overlay virtual characters, scenes, or information onto physical environments, creating interactive and immersive narratives. In the context of language, this opens up possibilities for language-rich storytelling experiences where users can engage with characters speaking different languages, explore linguistic diversity, and experience narratives that incorporate multilingual elements. This innovative approach to storytelling not only captivates audiences but also promotes language exploration and appreciation.

Although augmented reality in language offers many advantages, there are drawbacks and things to consider. The design of practical AR language applications requires careful attention to user experience, ensuring that the integration of digital overlays is manageable for users. Striking a balance between the virtual and physical elements is crucial to creating a seamless and engaging AR experience that enhances language learning and communication without causing cognitive overload.

Privacy concerns arise in the context of AR, mainly when devices are used to capture and analyze the user's surroundings. Language learning applications that use AR to analyze the user's environment for contextual learning may inadvertently capture sensitive information. Developers and educators must enact comprehensive privacy protocols, elucidate data usage guidelines, and guarantee that augmented reality applications precede user privacy and permission.

Technical challenges, such as the limitations of current AR hardware and the need for reliable tracking and recognition algorithms, also impact the effectiveness of AR language applications. Technological developments in augmented reality (AR), such as better device capabilities, better spatial mapping, and more precise object detection, will help improve and expand AR use in language-related applications.

Future directions for augmented reality in language provide promising opportunities. As AR hardware evolves, becoming more compact, powerful, and widely accessible, the integration of AR into everyday language experiences will likely become more seamless. The development of AR glasses with advanced features, including real-time language translation, interactive language exercises, and context-aware language support, could revolutionize how we engage with languages daily.

Integrating AI-driven language models with AR can result in more natural and context-aware language interactions. For example, AR devices with advanced language understanding algorithms could interpret user gestures, context, and spoken language to provide personalized language assistance, creating a more intuitive and responsive language learning experience.

Collaborative and social AR language experiences are also on the horizon. Users could participate in cooperative AR language activities, including language games, online language exchanges, or group study of linguistic and cultural materials. This social dimension adds an interpersonal aspect to language learning and communication, fostering collaboration and community-building among learners and speakers of different languages.

In summary, augmented reality has become a groundbreaking technology that will significantly impact communication, language acquisition, and language integration in physical environments. From immersive language learning experiences to real-time translation and cultural exploration, AR enriches our linguistic interactions with the world around us. As technology continues to evolve, the synergy between augmented reality and language holds the promise of unlocking new dimensions of linguistic exploration, promoting cross-cultural understanding, and enhancing our ability to communicate effectively in a multilingual and interconnected world.

**Potential Innovations on the Horizon**

As we stand at the intersection of various technological, scientific, and societal advancements, the horizon is teeming with potential innovations that promise to reshape our future. This section explores several areas of possible innovation on the horizon, spanning fields such as artificial intelligence, biotechnology, sustainable energy, space exploration, and the convergence of technology and human augmentation.

Artificial intelligence (AI) stands as a beacon of transformative potential on the horizon of innovation. AI development has significantly impacted several industries, including healthcare, banking, education, and entertainment. AI advancements can expand the capabilities of robots greatly in the future. Developing more advanced and ethical AI systems is crucial, emphasizing explainability, fairness, and transparency. Various advancements in machine learning, natural language processing, and neural networks hold the potential to create AI models that not only understand and generate human-like text but also exhibit a more profound comprehension of context, emotions, and nuanced communication.

Another field with a plethora of possible breakthroughs is biotechnology. Novel developments in gene editing technologies, such as CRISPR-Cas9, provide previously unattainable opportunities in genetic medicine, agriculture, and other fields. The ability to precisely edit DNA sequences has profound implications for treating genetic disorders, creating genetically modified organisms with enhanced traits, and even exploring the potential for human augmentation. The ethical considerations surrounding gene editing, including consent, equity, and unintended consequences, will be critical as these innovations move from the laboratory to practical applications.

Sustainable energy solutions are a pressing need for our planet, and the horizon holds promises of groundbreaking innovations in this domain. Developing next-generation renewable energy technologies, such as advanced solar panels, energy storage systems, and innovative approaches to harnessing wind, tidal, and geothermal energy, is crucial for transitioning toward a more sustainable and carbon-neutral future. Innovations in energy efficiency, grid management, and decentralized energy production could revolutionize how we generate, distribute, and consume energy, addressing the challenges of climate change and diminishing fossil fuel resources.

Space exploration continues to captivate the human imagination, and ambitious projects and technological advancements mark the horizon of innovation in this field. The potential for human settlement on Mars is a tempting prospect, with ongoing developments in space habitats, life support systems, and propulsion technologies. Innovations in space tourism, satellite technology, and deep-space exploration are reshaping our understanding of the cosmos and expanding the frontiers of human exploration. As private companies and international collaborations drive these innovations, the horizon of space exploration becomes increasingly accessible.

The convergence of technology and human augmentation is a frontier with transformative potential for enhancing human capabilities. Human-machine symbiosis is facilitated by advancements in neurotechnology, prostheses, and brain-computer interfaces, opening up new opportunities for people with disabilities. Developing brain-machine interfaces that enable direct communication between the human brain and external devices has implications for assistive technologies, cognitive enhancement, and immersive virtual experiences. Ethical considerations surrounding privacy, consent, and the potential for cognitive augmentation raise critical questions as these innovations advance.

In quantum computing, the horizon is illuminated by the potential for revolutionary advancements in computation power. Quantum computers, harnessing the principles of quantum mechanics, may resolve complex problems at speeds unattainable by classical computers. Developing scalable and error-tolerant quantum systems is a key focus, with implications for cryptography, optimization, and materials science. Computing on a quantum level can completely transform specific sectors. They are leading to drug discovery, climate modeling, and artificial intelligence breakthroughs.

The field of materials science is witnessing innovations that promise to redefine the materials we use in everyday life. Advanced materials with properties designed at the molecular or atomic level hold the potential to revolutionize industries such as electronics, transportation, healthcare, and construction. Innovations in nanotechnology, metamaterials, and biomimicry are paving the way for more robust, lighter, and versatile materials. As researchers explore the frontiers of material design, the horizon holds the potential for sustainable, high-performance materials that address global challenges.

Fusing virtual and augmented reality technologies creates immersive experiences beyond entertainment and gaming. The horizon of innovation in extended reality (XR) encompasses applications in education, healthcare, remote collaboration, and training. Innovations in haptic feedback, spatial computing, and photorealistic rendering contribute to more realistic and engaging XR experiences. As these technologies become more accessible, the potential for transformative changes in learning, working, and interacting in virtual environments is on the horizon.

The financial, governmental, and digital landscapes are changing due to blockchain and decentralized technologies. The potential for innovations in decentralized finance (DeFi), non-fungible tokens (NFTs), and blockchain-based identity systems is expanding. Smart contracts, which automate and enforce the terms of agreements without the need for intermediaries, hold promise for disrupting traditional legal and financial processes. With the development of blockchain technologies, new avenues for democratization, trust, and transparency are becoming available through decentralized apps and systems.

The intersection of robotics and artificial intelligence gives rise to innovations in autonomous systems and robotics applications. From autonomous vehicles and drones to robotic surgery and manufacturing, the potential for robotics to enhance efficiency and safety across various industries is vast. Innovations in soft robotics, swarm robotics, and human-robot collaboration are pushing the boundaries of what autonomous systems can achieve. As these technologies advance, the horizon holds the promise of robots seamlessly integrating into our daily lives, augmenting human capabilities, and performing tasks in diverse environments.

The continuous struggle between innovators and cyber dangers defines the future of cybersecurity. Advances in cybersecurity technologies, including AI-driven threat detection, quantum-resistant encryption, and decentralized identity solutions, are crucial for safeguarding digital assets and privacy. Innovations in cybersecurity practices, such as zero-trust architectures and secure-by-design principles, are becoming increasingly important in a world where cyber threats are growing in sophistication and scale.

Future breakthroughs could impact society, raise ethical questions, and require responsible technological development and use. Issues such as privacy, equity, bias, and the environmental footprint of technological advancements demand careful attention. As we navigate the horizon of innovation, it is imperative to consider not only the possibilities these innovations bring but also the ethical frameworks that guide their implementation for the benefit of humanity.

In conclusion, the horizon of innovation is a canvas painted with the brushstrokes of human curiosity, ingenuity, and the pursuit of progress. From artificial intelligence and biotechnology to sustainable energy, space exploration, and the convergence of technology and human augmentation, the potential innovations offer glimpses into a future where the boundaries of what is possible are continually pushed. As we stand on the cusp of these revolutionary breakthroughs, the responsible and ethical stewardship of innovation will determine the course of our collective voyage into the unknown future.

# Chapter 6

# Language and Human Connection

**Impact of Technology on Human Interaction**

The impact of technology on human interaction has been profound, reshaping how individuals connect, communicate, and engage with one another in both personal and professional spheres. As technology advances at an unprecedented pace, its influence on human interaction becomes increasingly complex, with positive and negative consequences. The purpose of this section is to investigate the myriad ways in which technology has influenced human contact. Specifically, we will explore how communication patterns have changed, the development of social interactions, the impact on mental health, and technology's role in fostering communication and isolation.

The way technology has changed human connection is most evident in how communication patterns have changed. How individuals communicate with one another has been fundamentally altered with the introduction of the internet, social media platforms, and instant messaging. Communication has become more instantaneous, transcending geographical boundaries and enabling real-time interactions. While this connectivity has facilitated global communication and collaboration, it has also altered the nature of interpersonal communication. In some instances, face-to-face conversations are supplanted by digital exchanges, leading to shifts in the dynamics of human connection.

Facebook, Twitter, and Instagram are examples of social media platforms widely used worldwide. Play a significant part in forming human interaction between individuals. These platforms allow individuals to share their lives, thoughts, and experiences with a vast audience. The idea of a "digital self" appears, in which people create an online persona that may differ from who they are in real life. This digital self, while providing a means of self-expression, also raises questions about authenticity and the impact of curated online identities on genuine human connection.

The widespread use of cell phones has made technology's influence on human connections even more pronounced. Mobile devices enable constant connectivity, allowing individuals to communicate anytime and anywhere. The lines between personal and work life are becoming more hazy, even as connectivity improves accessibility and communication. The phenomenon of "always being on" contributes to the erosion of traditional distinctions between work and leisure, impacting the quality of personal relationships and individual well-being.

Both enrichment and challenges mark the evolution of social relationships in the digital age. Social networks and online communities offer venues for people with similar interests to interact, promoting the development of international communities. However, the quality of these connections may differ from face-to-face relationships, as the digital realm needs more nuanced cues of non-verbal communication that contribute to understanding and empathy. The number of online connections may not necessarily translate into meaningful relationships, leading to a paradox where individuals may feel more connected yet experience increased loneliness and isolation.

As the panorama of human connection continues to evolve, one of the most important aspects to consider is technology's impact on mental health. The constant exposure to social media, online information, and the pressures of maintaining a digital presence contribute to the phenomenon of "technostress." Concerns about missing out (also known as FOMO) social comparison and the addictive nature of online platforms can contribute to anxiety, depression, and a sense of inadequacy. On the positive side, technology also serves as a tool for mental health support, with applications and platforms offering resources for mindfulness, therapy, and community engagement.

The emergence of online dating services is an example of how technology affects romantic relationships. These platforms offer people access to a broader range of possible mates but also bring new difficulties. The commodification of relationships, the emphasis on physical appearance, and the gamification of dating can contribute to a superficial approach to romance. People navigating the intricacies of internet dating may also need help due to the paradox of choice, which states that having too many alternatives can cause indecision.

Technology has brought about a significant alteration in the way people interact in schools. The advent of online learning platforms, virtual classrooms, and educational apps has expanded access to education globally. But the transition to digital learning also puts traditional classroom dynamics in jeopardy. The absence of face-to-face interactions, the potential for distractions, and the digital divide in access to technology create a complex landscape for educators and students alike. The impact of technology on education extends beyond formal settings, influencing informal learning through online communities and resources.

Another setting where technology affects how people interact in the workplace. Remote work, facilitated by digital communication tools, has become more prevalent, offering flexibility and opportunities for global collaboration. However, the virtual nature of remote work raises concerns about the loss of spontaneous interactions, team cohesion, and the potential for social isolation. The integration of artificial intelligence in the workforce introduces questions about the future of human-machine collaboration, emphasizing the importance of emotional intelligence and interpersonal skills in an increasingly digitized workplace.

The impact of technology on political and social interactions is evident in the era of digital activism and online movements. Social media platforms are hubs for information sharing, protest planning, and community mobilization. The democratization of information via digital platforms has given people the capacity to participate in public discourse and promote social change. But the same platforms may also reinforce echo chambers, polarize viewpoints, and aid in disseminating false information, undermining the notion of an informed and thoughtful public sphere.

Technology's role in fostering connectivity and isolation is a paradox that defines the contemporary human experience. Technology brings alienation and detachment even as it makes it possible for people to remain linked to a worldwide network. The prevalence of digital communication can lead to a sense of distance in face-to-face interactions, as individuals may prioritize virtual connections over in-person engagement. The paradox of being more connected than ever while experiencing increased feelings of isolation underscores the intricate relationship between technology and human interaction.

As we navigate the evolving landscape of technology-mediated human interaction, the need for a balanced and mindful approach becomes evident. A relevant and healthy digital society must consider how technology affects relationships, mental health, education, employment, and civic involvement. A more deliberate and thoughtful integration of technology into human contact can be achieved through fostering digital literacy, encouraging ethical technology use, and upholding a nuanced awareness of its advantages and disadvantages.

In conclusion, the impact of technology on human interaction is a dynamic and multifaceted phenomenon that shapes how we connect, communicate, and relate to one another. As we make the most of the possibilities and work towards overcoming the obstacles presented by technology, it is essential to approach its integration with a thoughtful consideration of its implications for relationships, mental well-being, and societal dynamics. Striking a balance between the virtual and the real, harnessing the benefits of technology while mitigating its potential drawbacks, is critical to fostering a future where technology enhances rather than diminishes the richness of human interaction.

## Maintaining Authentic Communication

Maintaining authentic communication in dominated by technology and digital interactions is a nuanced challenge that transcends the boundaries of personal and professional spheres. Authenticity, defined as genuine, truthful, and sincere, lies at the heart of meaningful human connections. The risk of losing authenticity is ever-present in the digital age, where communication often occurs through screens, devices, and platforms. This section analyzes the value of genuine communication and how technology affects authenticity. It provides advice on maintaining real connections in a world where virtual interactions are becoming more and more prevalent.

Sincere human connections are built on authentic communication, which promotes emotional resonance, comprehension, and trust. When individuals communicate authentically, they express their thoughts, feelings, and intentions sincerely, creating a foundation for meaningful relationships. In communication, authenticity entails being open, honest, and willing to share oneself. It goes beyond the superficial exchanges, allowing people to connect more deeply and authentically. In personal relationships, authenticity builds intimacy and fosters a sense of belonging, while in professional settings, it establishes credibility and promotes collaboration.

The emergence of digital communication technologies has brought up a range of prospects and obstacles to authenticity. On the one hand, technology facilitates instantaneous communication, breaking down geographical barriers and enabling connections across vast distances. Social media platforms, messaging apps, and video conferencing tools offer unprecedented ways to stay in touch, share experiences, and build communities. However, the very nature of digital communication poses challenges to maintaining authenticity. The curated nature of online personas, the brevity of text-based interactions, and the absence of non-verbal cues create a digital environment where authenticity can be easily obscured.

Social media, a ubiquitous force in contemporary communication, exemplifies the complexity of authenticity in the digital realm. Platforms like Facebook, Instagram, and Twitter provide individuals with tools to share their lives, thoughts, and experiences with a global audience. However, the pressure to present an idealized version of oneself, often driven by the desire for validation and social approval, can create curated online identities. The gap between the real and the projected self on social media raises questions about the authenticity of online interactions as individuals navigate the tension between genuine expression and the pursuit of a carefully crafted image.

The brevity of text-based communication, prevalent in email, instant messaging, and social media posts, poses a challenge to conveying authentic expression. With verbal and non-verbal cues, recovery is possible through the intricacies of tone, emotion, and context. Emojis and punctuation are attempts to inject emotion into digital messages, yet they may need to capture the richness of face-to-face communication. The risk of misinterpretation and misunderstanding looms large in text-based communication, highlighting the need for intentional efforts to convey authenticity in digital interactions.

Although it adds a visual element to communication, video conferencing poses additional difficulties for authenticity. "Zoom fatigue" is a phenomenon that highlights the strain that comes with extended virtual meetings and the work that goes into projecting authentic participation across screens. The inability of digital communication technologies to replicate the natural flow and spontaneity of in-person talks highlights the significance of deliberate tactics for maintaining authenticity in online encounters.

Retaining authenticity in the workplace is crucial for collaborative teamwork, effective leadership, and corporate culture. Authentic leaders inspire trust and loyalty, fostering a positive workplace environment. The shift to remote work, accelerated by global events, has amplified the need for authentic leadership in virtual settings. Leaders who authentically communicate their values, vision, and concerns create a sense of connection and stability in the digital workplace. Transparency communication about obstacles, doubts, and accomplishments fosters a culture of openness and trust. This reduces the possibility of misunderstandings and promotes a cohesive virtual team.

Organizational communication demands intentional efforts to preserve authenticity, particularly in remote work. The absence of physical proximity in virtual workplaces underscores the need for clear, empathetic, and transparent communication. Authenticity in organizational communication involves acknowledging the human aspects of work, recognizing individual contributions, and fostering a sense of community despite geographical dispersion. Strategies such as virtual town halls, regular check-ins, and the use of video messages from leadership contribute to a more authentic organizational communication landscape.

Maintaining authenticity in digital communication necessitates a deliberate strategy that capitalizes on the medium's advantages while appreciating its drawbacks. One critical method is to prioritize active listening in virtual interactions. Despite screen' obstacles, people can foster a genuine connection by being present, focused, and receptive in virtual interactions. Acknowledging and validating the perspectives of others, even in the absence of physical cues, contributes to a sense of being heard and understood, fostering authenticity in communication.

The intentional use of storytelling is another powerful tool for preserving authenticity in digital communication. Tales can eloquently and relatably communicate feelings, experiences, and morals. Whether in a professional presentation, a social media post, or an email, incorporating personal narratives adds a human touch to digital communication. Authentic storytelling transcends the formalities of virtual communication, creating a shared space for connection and understanding.

Building authentic connections in the digital realm also involves being mindful of language choices. The written word, devoid of vocal intonation and body language, requires careful consideration to convey tone accurately. Digital messages are more authentic when they use language that means sincerity, empathy, and genuine interest. Additionally, expressing vulnerability, when appropriate, fosters a climate of openness and authenticity, allowing individuals to connect on a deeper level.

Retaining authenticity in communication requires striking a balance between digital and in-person interactions. While face-to-face encounters bring depth and complexity that can be difficult to recreate electronically, digital communication can be more convenient and accessible. Video calls should be included. They help people connect more genuinely because they record gestures, facial expressions, and other small communication details.

Developing digital etiquette is essential to maintaining authenticity in online relationships. Respectful and considerate communication, adherence to professional norms, and a mindful approach to digital expression contribute to a positive and authentic online environment. Embracing digital etiquette involves recognizing the impact of one's words and actions on others, fostering a sense of community, and upholding ethical standards in the digital realm.

Educating individuals on the nuances of digital communication and the potential pitfalls of misinterpretation is a proactive strategy for maintaining authenticity. Participants in training courses and workshops that emphasize effective digital communication techniques, such as tone control, active listening, and virtual presence, are better equipped to handle the complexities of online interactions genuinely and understandably. Stressing the human element of digital communication inspires people to approach online contacts with compassion and a sincere desire to establish a connection.

In summary, preserving genuine connection in the digital age necessitates a thoughtful and deliberate approach that acknowledges the potential and difficulties brought about by technology. Authenticity, a crucial component of deep human connections, may still be attained in virtual encounters using techniques like conscious language selection, storytelling, attentive listening, and striking a balance between digital and in-person communication. Preserving authenticity in personal relationships, professional settings, and organizational contexts contributes to a more genuine, empathetic, and connected digital landscape. As we navigate the evolving terrain of digital communication, the enduring value of authenticity serves as a guiding principle for fostering meaningful connections in an increasingly virtual world.

**Overcoming Challenges in the Digital Age**

In the digital age, opportunities that were previously unimaginable have emerged. And efficiencies, transforming how we live, work, and connect. But there are drawbacks to this age of technical growth as well. Because digital technologies are becoming increasingly dependent on civilization, individuals and organizations grapple with various issues, from privacy concerns to the digital divide. This section examines the problems that the digital age has brought about. It suggests ways to overcome them to ensure a more ethical, safe, and inclusive digital future.

One of the foremost challenges in the digital age revolves around the issue of privacy. The extensive collection and utilization of personal data by online platforms, social media, and tech companies raise profound concerns about safeguarding individuals' privacy. Because data-driven technologies are so widely used, there is a greater awareness of the need for strong privacy measures, as seen by incidents like targeted advertising and data breaches. Finding a middle ground between the conveniences given by personalized services and the protection of user privacy is a delicate challenge that demands regulatory frameworks, transparent practices, and informed consent mechanisms.

Cybersecurity emerges as a critical challenge in the digital age, as the interconnected nature of digital systems exposes individuals, businesses, and governments to cyber threats. The weaknesses of digital infrastructures provide severe threats to data security and integrity, ranging from ransomware assaults to identity theft. Strong cybersecurity defenses are essential, such as threat detection systems, encryption, and safe authentication procedures. Additionally, cultivating a cybersecurity awareness and education culture is crucial in empowering individuals to protect themselves and their digital assets.

The digital divide is a significant obstacle that makes social injustices worse. While digital technologies offer immense opportunities for education, employment, and access to information, a substantial portion of the global population remains digitally marginalized. Inequalities in infrastructure, technological literacy, and internet access create a divide that prevents people and communities from taking full advantage of the advantages of the digital age. Bridging the digital divide requires concerted efforts to provide affordable access to technology, digital skills training, and inclusive policies that ensure equitable participation in the digital ecosystem.

Misinformation and spreading fake news pose significant challenges in the digital age, impacting public discourse, trust in information sources, and democratic processes. The rapid dissemination of information through online platforms, coupled with algorithms prioritizing engagement over accuracy, creates an environment where misinformation can proliferate. Combatting this challenge requires a multifaceted approach involving media literacy education, fact-checking initiatives, responsible platform algorithms, and public awareness campaigns to equip individuals with the ability to think critically, which is necessary for navigating the digital information landscape.

An increasing problem in the digital age is digital addiction and usage, especially when it comes to social media and online entertainment. The addictive design elements incorporated into digital platforms, such as infinite scrolling and notifications, contribute to compulsive behaviors and negative impacts on mental well-being. Addressing digital addiction involves individual responsibility and collective efforts from technology companies to design platforms prioritizing user well-being. Encouraging mindful technology use, fostering digital detox practices, and promoting a healthy balance between online and offline activities are essential to overcoming this challenge.

The rapid pace of technological innovation introduces challenges related to job displacement and the evolving nature of employment. Automation, artificial intelligence, and robotics have the potential to reshape industries and job markets, leading to workforce disruptions. Preparing for the future of work involves spending money on educational and training programs that provide people with the tools they need to succeed in emerging job sectors. Additionally, fostering a culture of adaptability and lifelong learning is essential for navigating the dynamic landscape of employment in the digital age.

E-waste and environmental sustainability present pressing challenges associated with the proliferation of electronic devices and the rapid turnover of technology. The disposal of obsolete electronic equipment contributes to environmental pollution and resource depletion. Implementing responsible e-waste management practices, promoting the recycling and refurbishment of electronic devices, and designing products with longevity and sustainability are crucial steps in mitigating the environmental impact of the digital age.

Ensuring the ethical development and deployment of emerging technologies, including biotechnology and artificial intelligence, is a complex challenge that requires careful consideration. Ethical dilemmas surrounding algorithmic bias, privacy infringements, and the potential misuse of advanced technologies underscore the importance of establishing ethical guidelines, regulatory frameworks, and industry standards. Encouraging interdisciplinary collaborations involving ethicists, technologists, policymakers, and the public is essential in addressing the ethical challenges that accompany technological advancements.

The erosion of face-to-face communication and the prevalence of digital interactions present challenges to interpersonal relationships and community bonds. Even though screen-mediated communication allows for connections beyond geographic boundaries, it can also exacerbate feelings of loneliness, depersonalization, and a lack of genuine connection. Mitigating this challenge involves intentionally balancing digital communication with face-to-face interactions, fostering digital literacy for meaningful online engagement, and cultivating a sense of community in physical and digital spaces.

Overcoming the obstacles of the digital era necessitates a comprehensive and cooperative strategy involving people, communities, companies, governments, and tech developers. Regulatory frameworks that prioritize user privacy, cybersecurity, and ethical considerations are foundational in creating a secure and transparent digital environment. Education and awareness campaigns that promote digital literacy, critical thinking, and responsible technology empower individuals to navigate the digital landscape effectively.

Initiatives to bridge the digital divide must address infrastructural barriers, affordability issues, and disparities in digital literacy. Governments, nonprofits, and businesses can work together to guarantee that underprivileged populations are not left behind in the digital revolution and to give fair access to technology. Additionally, efforts to combat misinformation require partnerships between media organizations, fact-checking agencies, and technology platforms to promote accurate information and media literacy.

Addressing environmental concerns associated with the digital age involves sustainable practices in product design, responsible e-waste management, and the promotion of circular economy principles. Leaders in the industry are crucial in promoting sustainable methods of producing and consuming technology and embracing eco-friendly practices. Public awareness campaigns can also encourage consumers to make environmentally conscious choices in using and disposing of electronic devices.

Overcoming challenges related to digital addiction requires a collective commitment to promoting healthy technology habits. Individuals should adopt conscious behaviors like limiting screen time, taking digital breaks, and promoting in-person relationships, while technology businesses can make design modifications that promote user well-being. Education and awareness campaigns on the impact of digital addiction contribute to building a culture that values the balance between technology use and overall well-being.

Collaboration between corporations, governments, and educational institutions regarding employment and workforce concerns is crucial. Investing in education and upskilling programs that align with the needs of emerging industries ensures that individuals are equipped for the jobs of the future. Businesses can implement inclusive hiring practices and support ongoing professional development, while governments can enact policies that encourage workforce resilience and adaptation to technological shifts.

The ethical implications of developing technologies demand a global dialogue among researchers, industry executives, legislators, and the general public. Establishing ethical guidelines, transparency in technological development, and accountability mechanisms are critical in shaping the responsible use of advanced technologies. Constant communication and interdisciplinary teamwork can foster a shared awareness of the digital era's moral dilemmas and possible remedies.

Preserving face-to-face communication and fostering genuine connections amidst the prevalence of digital interactions requires a cultural shift. People can intentionally prioritize face-to-face communication, establish limits on digital communication, and foster relationships offline. Businesses and organizations can promote workplace cultures that value virtual and physical connection, fostering environments beyond the digital realm where employees feel seen, heard, and loved.

To sum up, the digital age's problems are complex and ever-changing, necessitating creative and cooperative solutions.

Addressing issues such as privacy, cybersecurity, the digital divide, misinformation, digital addiction, employment shifts, environmental sustainability, and ethical considerations becomes paramount as technology advances. Society may traverse the digital era with resilience by adopting a holistic strategy encompassing individuals, communities, corporations, and legislators. This will help to mitigate any adverse effects of technology while maximizing its positive aspects. Pursuing a balanced, inclusive, and ethically grounded digital future is essential for shaping a world where technology serves humanity in a positive and transformative manner.

## Chapter 7

## Ethical Considerations in Language Unleashed

**Privacy Concerns**

Privacy concerns have emerged as a central issue in the digital age, fueled by the extensive collection, analysis, and utilization of personal information facilitated by advanced technologies. The proliferation of online platforms, mobile applications, and connected devices has ushered in unprecedented conveniences. Still, it has also created a complex landscape where the boundaries between public and private spheres are increasingly blurred. The digital ecosystem, driven by data-driven business models, has ignited a discourse on the ethical implications of surveillance, data mining, and the commodification of personal information. As individuals navigate this interconnected landscape, they grapple with preserving their privacy in an era where news has become a valuable currency.

The widespread practice of data gathering by tech corporations, social media platforms, and other internet services is one of the main drivers of privacy concerns. Each click, search term, location check-in, and digital engagement generates a trail of carefully collected and examined data. This data, often called big data, serves as the lifeblood of targeted advertising, personalized recommendations, and algorithmic decision-making. Although these features improve convenience and user experience, a substantial amount of privacy is given up by users in exchange for them. The sheer volume and granularity of collected data raise questions about how individuals can maintain control over their personal information and whether informed consent is genuinely achievable in a world of complex data ecosystems.

Social media platforms, in particular, have become focal points for privacy concerns due to their central role in shaping online interactions and information sharing. Users willingly share a wealth of personal details, preferences, and even emotions on these platforms, often unaware of the far-reaching consequences. The Cambridge Analytica scandal, where user data was allegedly harvested without consent for political profiling, underscored the vulnerability of personal information within the social media landscape. The inherent tension between the desire to connect, share, and express oneself and the need to safeguard sensitive information highlights the challenges individuals face in navigating the privacy landscape of social media.

The rise of governmental and corporate surveillance technologies has further intensified privacy concerns. Closed-circuit television (CCTV) cameras, facial recognition systems, and location-tracking technologies have become ubiquitous in public spaces, causing problems over the harmonious relationship between safety and individual privacy. Government monitoring activities frequently carried out in the name of national security spark discussions regarding the limits of government intrusion into personal life. The tension between the need for public safety and the right to privacy underscores the delicate balance that policymakers must strike to address evolving threats while safeguarding civil liberties.

The commodification of personal information has transformed individuals into products, with their data serving as valuable assets in the digital economy. Data brokerage has become a lucrative industry where companies buy and sell consumer data for targeted advertising and market research. This secondary market for personal information operates primarily without individuals' knowledge or explicit consent, raising ethical concerns about commercializing private lives. The data brokerage ecosystem's lack of transparency and accountability exacerbates privacy anxieties as individuals realize that their personal information is traded as a commodity in an invisible marketplace.

Privacy concerns extend beyond online interactions to connected devices and the Internet of Things (IoT). Wearables, smart home appliances, smartphones, and other Internet of Things devices always gather data about users' habits, tastes, and health parameters. The interconnected nature of these devices creates an expansive network of data points that, when aggregated, can paint a comprehensive picture of an individual's life. The possibility of illegal access, breaches of data, and other security risks and misuse of sensitive information heightens the risks associated with the increasing integration of IoT into daily life. As smart cities and smart homes become more prevalent, the challenge lies in developing robust security measures and privacy safeguards to protect individuals from unwarranted intrusions.

Legislation and regulatory frameworks are crucial in addressing privacy concerns and establishing a foundation for responsible data practices. A regulation in the European Union known as a significant step forward is the General Data Protection Regulation (GDPR), a landmark effort to empower individuals with greater control over their data. It mandates transparent data processing practices, requires explicit consent for data collection, and imposes strict penalties for non-compliance. While GDPR has set a precedent for data protection globally, variations in privacy laws across jurisdictions create challenges for multinational companies operating in different regions. Harmonizing international data protection and privacy standards remains an ongoing challenge as the digital landscape continues to evolve.

Digital literacy and awareness are inextricably tied to privacy problems. Many people may unwittingly jeopardize their privacy because they are unaware of the methods by which their information is gathered, handled, and used. Individuals can make educated decisions about their online activities, recognize potential hazards, and apply steps that enhance their privacy when educational initiatives that promote digital literacy are implemented. Incorporating digital literacy into academic curricula, providing accessible resources for users of all ages, and fostering a culture of responsible digital citizenship are critical steps in addressing the root causes of privacy concerns.

PETs, which stand for privacy-enhancing technologies, are now being developed and adopted to represent a proactive approach to addressing privacy concerns in the digital age. Decentralized technology, encryption, and anonymous surfing tools provide more control over one's digital footprint and communication channels. Search engines and messaging apps that promote privacy prioritize user privacy and data security. As awareness of privacy issues grows, the demand for products and services that prioritize user privacy will likely increase, prompting technological innovation in the direction of privacy-centric solutions.

Organizational transparency and accountability are pivotal in building and maintaining trust with users concerned about privacy. Companies prioritizing ethical data practices, transparent privacy policies, and user-friendly consent mechanisms are more likely to engender trust among their user base. A proactive approach to addressing privacy problems is represented by the concept of privacy-by-design, which includes privacy considerations in developing products and services from the beginning of the process. By putting the onus on organizations to prioritize user privacy, individuals can feel more confident in their interactions within the digital landscape.

The dynamic terrain of privacy issues in the digital era demands constant communication between all relevant parties, such as legislators, tech companies, privacy advocates, and members of the public. Candid conversations about the moral implications of data activities, the boundaries of surveillance, and the duties of tech businesses foster a shared awareness of the complex nature of privacy problems. Involving multiple stakeholders can help create industry standards and fair laws safeguarding people's privacy while promoting technological innovation and economic expansion.

In conclusion, privacy concerns in the digital age are complex, multifaceted, and dynamic. As individuals, organizations, and policymakers navigate this evolving landscape, it is essential to strike a delicate balance between the advantages of technological advancement and the preservation of individual privacy. Through robust legislation, educational initiatives, privacy-enhancing technologies, organizational transparency, and open dialogues, society can work toward creating a digital environment where privacy is respected, protected, and valued. As we confront the challenges of the digital age, a commitment to upholding privacy rights becomes imperative for building a future where individuals can participate in the digital world with confidence and autonomy.

## Bias in Language Technology

Bias in language technology is a pervasive and complex issue that reflects and perpetuates societal inequalities. Natural language processing (NLP) models and machine learning algorithms are examples of language technologies that have become essential components of various applications. These technologies include virtual assistants and automated decision-making systems. As technology continues to play an increasingly integral role in shaping human interactions, language technologies have become increasingly important. However, these technologies often inherit and amplify biases in the data they are trained, raising ethical concerns about fairness, accountability, and the potential reinforcement of societal inequalities.

Language technology, particularly NLP models, relies heavily on large datasets for training. The language patterns and subtleties in the data, which are generally derived from various web content, are captured by these datasets. The Internet, however, is not accessible from the prejudices that permeate all human societies. Historical prejudices, stereotypes, and societal imbalances are reflected in online language. When these biased datasets are used to train language models, the models learn and reproduce the biases present in the data, perpetuating existing inequalities.

One prominent example of bias in language technology is the reproduction of gender bias. When trained on diverse datasets, many language models have exhibited gender stereotypes, associating certain professions or roles with specific genders. This is an example of the gender bias that has kept some people from achieving their full potential in society. For instance, a model trained on biased data might associate words like "nurse" with women and "engineer" with men, reinforcing traditional gender roles.

Ethnic and racial biases are also prevalent in language technology. It is possible for models trained on online text data to acquire and sustain racial and ethnic preconceptions unknowingly. Because of this, language predictions and categorizations may become prejudiced, reflecting past biases. For example, an NLP model might associate certain words or phrases with specific racial or ethnic groups, leading to discriminatory outcomes in applications like automated content moderation or sentiment analysis.

The impact of biased language technology extends beyond perpetuating stereotypes; it can have real-world consequences, especially in applications involving automated decision-making. It is possible for algorithms driven by language models to inadvertently discriminate against specific populations in industries like banking, law enforcement, and employment. For instance, biased language models can contribute to discriminatory outcomes in resume screening, leading to the exclusion of candidates based on gender, race, or other protected characteristics.

Addressing bias in language technology requires a multifaceted approach encompassing data collection, model training, and ongoing evaluation. Efforts to reduce prejudice should start by seriously considering the training datasets. Data collection processes should aim to be inclusive and representative, covering diverse voices, perspectives, and linguistic variations. It is also essential to seek out biases in current datasets and fix them so everyone has a fair chance.

A key component in reducing bias is the creation and improvement of algorithms. Researchers and engineers must devise methods to identify and mitigate biases when training. Techniques such as debiasing algorithms, adversarial training, and attention to fairness metrics can contribute to creating more equitable language models. Additionally, continuous monitoring and evaluation of model performance across diverse demographic groups are essential to identify and address biases that may emerge during deployment.

To combat bias in language technologies, openness is critical. Developers and organizations must be transparent about the data sources, methodologies, and decision-making processes in creating language models. Providing insights into the potential biases present in the models fosters accountability and enables external scrutiny. Open-sourcing models and making their underlying code accessible to the public can facilitate collaborative efforts to identify and rectify biases.

To reduce bias, it is crucial to be inclusive during development. Team members developing language models should reflect the communities they are trying to serve and come from various backgrounds and experiences. To create language technologies that are more equitable and inclusive, it is essential to have a diverse workforce that can recognize and comprehend the subtle forms of bias.

Education and awareness are essential components of addressing bias in language technology. Users and developers alike need to be informed about the potential preferences in language models and the ethical implications of their use. Training programs should emphasize responsible AI practices, ethical considerations, and the societal impacts of biased language technologies. Developers can contribute to a more informed and conscientious approach to deploying language technology by fostering an awareness culture.

Government regulations and industry standards also play a crucial role in addressing bias in language technology. Legislation requiring openness, equity, and responsibility in creating and using language models can be passed by governing and regulating organizations. Industry standards can guide ethical AI practices, encouraging organizations to adopt responsible approaches to language technology development.

The role of the broader artificial intelligence (AI) community is integral in the collective effort to address bias. When researchers, practitioners, and policymakers work together, they can share what has worked and hasn't and how to tackle prejudice more effectively. Conferences, workshops, and forums dedicated to fairness in AI provide platforms for interdisciplinary discussions and the dissemination of research findings.

There has been a lot of progress in identifying and fixing prejudice in language tech, but there are still a lot of obstacles. The dynamic and evolving nature of language and the intricacies of human communication make eradicating bias a formidable task. However, ongoing study, development, and collaboration can pave the way for significant advancements in mitigating bias in language technology.

In conclusion, bias in language technology is a multifaceted challenge that requires concerted efforts from researchers, developers, policymakers, and the broader AI community. Recognizing and rectifying biases in language models is crucial for creating fair and equitable technology and preventing the perpetuation of societal inequalities. Through inclusive data practices, algorithmic refinements, transparency, education, and regulatory frameworks, the AI community can contribute to building language technologies that reflect the diversity of human expression while upholding ethical standards and societal values. To ensure that language technology develops in a way that values and promotes inclusion and fairness, addressing bias is society's duty as much as a technical one.

## Responsible Development and Use of Language Tools

To successfully traverse the ever-changing terrain of AI and NLP, building and deploying language tools responsibly is crucial. As language technologies become integral to various aspects of daily life, from virtual assistants to automated content moderation, ethical considerations surrounding their design, deployment, and impact on society come to the forefront. Ethical concerns, openness, inclusivity, and continuous evaluation are all part of a holistic approach to responsible development. This essay explores the fundamental principles of responsible development and use of language tools, examining the ethical challenges, the role of transparency, the importance of inclusivity, and the necessity of continuous evaluation in ensuring that language technologies contribute positively to society.

When it comes to developing language tools responsibly, ethical issues are crucial. Language models and NLP algorithms have the potential to shape human interactions, influence decision-making processes, and impact societal norms. Therefore, developers must prioritize ethical principles to prevent unintended consequences and negative societal impacts. One significant moral concern is the perpetuation of biases within language technologies. Prejudice, whether gender, racial, or cultural, can be inadvertently embedded in training data, leading to biased predictions and outcomes. Careful dataset curation, algorithmic modifications, and continuing reviews are crucial in reducing biases, and responsible developers understand this. By addressing biases, developers contribute to creating language tools that align with principles of fairness, justice, and inclusivity.

Transparency is a foundation of responsible development, which helps build confidence among developers, users, and the public. Users have the right to understand how language tools operate, how they make predictions, and how they handle sensitive information. Developers should prioritize clear communication about the data sources, methodologies, and decision-making processes involved in creating language models. Making code available to the public and using open-sourcing approaches increase openness, allowing for external analysis and collaborative efforts to find any problems. Transparent practices build trust and empower users to make informed decisions about using language tools, fostering a sense of agency in the digital landscape.

Making sure that language tools are inclusive is crucial for meeting the different demands of users all across the world. The development process should include perspectives from a broad range of demographics to avoid the unintentional marginalization of certain groups. Inclusive language tools recognize linguistic variations, dialects, and cultural nuances, avoiding a one-size-fits-all approach. Developers should strive to create models that understand and respect diverse forms of expression, accommodating users from different linguistic backgrounds. By prioritizing inclusivity, language tools become more accessible, equitable, and relevant to a broad spectrum of users, contributing to a more democratic and representative digital space.

Conscious application of technology and ethical creation of linguistic tools are inseparable. Users, developers, and policymakers all play roles in ensuring that language tools are applied ethically and do not contribute to harm. Developers should design tools with ethical use in mind, incorporating safeguards against misuse and unintended consequences. Policymakers can enact regulations that set standards for ethical AI practices and provide guidelines for the responsible deployment of language technologies. The onus is on users to consider the consequences of their language tool choices and to push for ethical behavior. Responsible use requires a collective commitment to ethical principles, acknowledging the societal impact of language technologies, and actively working towards positive contributions to the digital landscape.

Responsible creation and use of linguistic tools requires continuous review. The dynamic nature of language and the ever-evolving digital landscape necessitate ongoing scrutiny of language models and algorithms. Regular evaluations help identify emerging issues, assess the impact of language tools on users and communities, and refine models to address evolving ethical considerations. Regular audits, feedback from broad user groups, and vigilance against any biases or unforeseen repercussions are all hallmarks of responsible development. Continuous evaluation ensures that language tools adapt to users' changing needs and expectations while upholding ethical standards and principles.

Reducing the adverse effects of language tools on the environment is a crucial part of sustainable development. The computational power required to train large language models contributes significantly to carbon emissions and energy consumption. Developers should explore energy-efficient training methods, optimize model architectures, and consider the environmental implications of their work. To ensure that technological improvements do not lead to ecological damage, it is essential to use resources responsibly, corresponding with larger sustainability goals.

Responsible development and use of language tools also entail considerations of user privacy. Language models often process large amounts of personal data, and users must have confidence that their information is handled carefully and by privacy regulations. Developers should implement robust privacy measures, such as data anonymization and encryption, and be transparent about data handling practices. Users, in turn, should be informed about the privacy implications of using language tools and have the option to control the extent to which their data is processed.

If we want AI and NLP to impact society positively in the future, we must ensure that they are developed and used responsibly. When creating and implementing language technologies, it is crucial to remember the following principles: openness, inclusivity, responsibility, assessment, sustainability, ethics, and user privacy. As the capabilities of language tools continue to advance, a commitment to responsible practices becomes paramount in ensuring that these technologies enhance human experiences, promote fairness, and contribute to a more inclusive and equitable digital world. By prioritizing responsible development, the AI community can pave the way for a future where language technologies align with societal values, prioritize user well-being, and foster a digital landscape that reflects the diversity of human expression and thought.

# Chapter 8

# Language Unleashed in Education

**Transforming Language Learning**

Language learning has undergone a remarkable transformation in recent years, fueled by advancements in technology, innovative pedagogical approaches, and a growing recognition of the importance of multilingualism in our interconnected world. This change encompasses more than just the methods and instruments used; it also involves a more comprehensive rethinking of language learning. As we delve into the various dimensions of this metamorphosis, it becomes evident that the traditional paradigms of language education are giving way to a more dynamic and personalized landscape.

As a field, language learning has been dramatically impacted by the incorporation of technology into teaching methods. Many language learning apps and websites are available now because computers, tablets, and smartphones are everywhere. These digital tools allow learners to engage with language materials at their own pace and offer interactive and immersive experiences. These environments enable learners to practice their language abilities in realistic scenarios, improving their competency and the belief that they can communicate in the language they are learning.

Furthermore, AI has become a revolutionary force in language instruction. AI-driven language learning platforms can adapt to students' needs and learning styles, providing customized learning experiences. Through natural language processing, AI can analyze linguistic patterns, identify areas of improvement, and offer targeted feedback. This personalized approach not only accelerates the learning process but also addresses the diverse needs of learners, making language acquisition more inclusive and effective.

The methods used to teach languages are also undergoing a radical change, and this isn't limited to the online world. The traditional emphasis on rote memorization and grammar drills gradually gives way to communicative and task-based approaches. Students are encouraged to utilize the language for practical purposes as part of communicative language training, which focuses on improving the ability to communicate successfully in real-life circumstances. Conversely, task-based language instruction makes language acquisition more contextual and engaging by incorporating it with relevant tasks.

The importance of considering cultural factors when teaching a language has also grown. Language encompasses more than just a collection of grammatical rules and vocabulary; it is also intricately connected to culture. Understanding cultural subtleties, idiomatic idioms, and social conventions is integral to a life-altering language-learning journey. Cultural competence is increasingly seen as an essential aspect of language proficiency, as it enables learners to navigate diverse social contexts and communicate with cultural sensitivity.

It is also impossible to exaggerate the importance of teachers in this life-altering process. Teachers now play a more active role as guides and facilitators, helping students navigate the complexities of language acquisition instead of just conveying information. The flipped classroom model, where students engage with instructional content at home and collaborative activities in the classroom, has gained traction. Through this method, students can actively participate in their education, and instructors can better meet their unique needs through tailored instruction.

The revolution in language acquisition is not limited to classrooms; it permeates non-academic contexts and continues throughout a person's life. More and more people are adopting a growth mentality, which sees language acquisition as an ongoing process. Online language communities, language exchange programs, and virtual language meetups enable learners to connect with native speakers and fellow learners worldwide, fostering a global language-learning ecosystem.

To sum up, the evolution of language acquisition is a complex process involving changing how people learn and teach and incorporating new technologies and pedagogical approaches. The importance of language in promoting international understanding and cooperation has been more widely acknowledged, and this change reflects that. It is crucial to embrace diverse techniques and keep researching new ways to make language learning more than just a skill acquisition process; it should be a rich and transforming experience. As we go through this changed terrain, this must be our goal.

## AI in Education

By posing further questions about established practices and paving the way for more tailored educational possibilities, artificial intelligence (AI) is revolutionizing how schools operate. We are seeing that AI is more than just a tool; it's a powerful force that can change the fundamentals of how knowledge is taught and learned as we move through this convergence of technology and education.

One of the most impactful applications of AI in education lies in personalized learning. When accommodating individual pupils' varied educational requirements, traditional classroom settings frequently require assistance. Nevertheless, artificial intelligence can analyze vast volumes of data, including students' learning habits, strengths, and shortcomings. Through machine learning algorithms, AI systems can adapt instructional content in real-time, tailoring it to each student's pace and style of learning. By catering to each student's requirements, this individualized method improves comprehension and promotes a more welcoming classroom climate.

Intelligent teaching systems, made possible by AI, provide students with online instructors who can provide them with real-time comments and pointers. These programs use NLP and ML to decipher students' questions and misunderstandings and provide personalized feedback. The continuous feedback loop created by intelligent tutoring systems not only aids in the mastery of subject matter but also cultivates a sense of self-directed learning as students receive real-time insights into their progress and areas requiring improvement.

Another significant stride AI makes in education is performing administrative chores through automation, a liberating crucial time for educators. Grading assignments, managing schedules, and administrative paperwork can take time, diverting educators' focus from teaching itself. AI-powered tools can streamline these processes, allowing teachers to invest more time interacting with students, developing innovative teaching methods, and providing individualized attention. This change from administrative work to active learning can transform teaching into a more satisfying and fruitful career path.

Furthermore, AI has opened avenues for developing innovative content and interactive learning materials. It is now possible to dynamically modify educational content according to the learner's preferences and progress. For instance, adaptive learning platforms use AI algorithms to assess a student's proficiency and adjust the difficulty level of exercises accordingly. This ensures learners are consistently challenged optimally, preventing boredom or frustration and promoting sustained engagement with the material.

Beyond the classroom, AI is affecting data-driven decision-making and educational research. Researchers can leverage AI algorithms to analyze vast datasets, identifying trends and patterns that may have been overlooked through traditional methods. This data-driven approach allows educators and policymakers to make informed decisions, from curriculum design to resource allocation, ensuring that educational interventions are evidence-based and tailored to the evolving needs of students.

There are a lot of advantages to using AI in the classroom, but there are also some obstacles. Privacy concerns, ethical considerations, and the digital divide are among the complex issues that need careful navigation. Safeguarding student data, ensuring transparency in AI algorithms, and bridging the gap in access to technology are critical aspects that demand attention. As we harness the power of AI, it is imperative to establish ethical frameworks and guidelines that prioritize the well-being and equity of all students.

Looking ahead, the role of educators in this AI-infused educational landscape becomes even more pivotal. Instead of being supplanted by machines, educators assume the role of conductors in a hybrid classroom, where human knowledge and AI work in tandem. The interpersonal skills, creativity, and skills teachers bring are irreplaceable. The symbiotic relationship between AI and educators promises to release the potential available to each student, fostering a generation equipped with academic knowledge, critical thinking skills, and adaptability.

 It is not merely about automating tasks or enhancing efficiency; it is about redefining the educational experience, making it more personalized, adaptive, and inclusive. We must find a way to use AI's powers while still being true to the ethical ideals that support fair and successful education as we go forward on this revolutionary path.

The collaboration between human educators and artificial intelligence heralds a future where education is not just about acquiring information but about nurturing the holistic development of individuals in a rapidly evolving world.

**Future Perspectives on Linguistic Education**

As we plot a path into the future, the field of language teaching is poised for revolutionary shifts. In this era of global connectivity and rapid technological advancement, the way we approach language learning is undergoing a paradigm shift. The future perspectives on linguistic education are shaped by a convergence of factors, including technological innovations, evolving pedagogical approaches, and a deepening understanding of the interconnectedness between language and culture.

Using state-of-the-art technology will be a defining feature of language teaching in the future. There will soon be a dramatic shift in how people learn languages thanks to AI, VR, and AR advancements. AI-driven language learning platforms, equipped with natural language processing capabilities, can provide individuals with personalized and adaptive learning journeys. These platforms analyze linguistic patterns, offer real-time feedback, and customize content based on the learner's proficiency and preferences, ushering in an era of tailored language education that caters to diverse needs.

Thanks to VR's ability to immerse users, students can experience real-life language settings without leaving the classroom. This experiential learning approach enables students to practice language skills in realistic scenarios, fostering cultural competence alongside linguistic proficiency. Augmented reality complements traditional language learning materials by overlaying digital information onto the physical world, creating interactive and dynamic learning experiences. As these technologies evolve, linguistic education is poised to become more engaging, efficient, and closely aligned with the demands of our interconnected global society.

Moreover, the future of linguistic education embraces a departure from traditional instructional methods towards more communicative and task-based approaches. The focus moves from cramming for tests and exams to using the language in everyday situations. Communicative language teaching encourages students to engage in meaningful conversations, emphasizing fluency and effective communication over strict adherence to grammatical structures. Task-based language teaching integrates language learning with purposeful tasks, connecting linguistic skills to practical applications. This shift not only enhances language proficiency but also equips learners with the ability to navigate diverse linguistic landscapes with confidence and versatility.

Developing students' cultural competence is quickly becoming essential to language curricula. Language is inherently intertwined with culture, and understanding the cultural context enriches language learning. Future language instruction programs will heavily explore cultural nuance, colloquial idioms, and social standards. This holistic approach deepens language comprehension and fosters cross-cultural understanding and communication. As we prepare learners for a world where global interactions are the norm, cultural sensitivity becomes integral to linguistic proficiency.

The role of educators in shaping the future of linguistic education cannot be overstated. In the evolving landscape, teachers are not merely disseminators of information; they are facilitators, mentors, and guides. Beyond the classroom, teachers are responsible for building an engaging and inclusive learning environment, integrating technology, and curating digital resources. Professional development programs for educators will be vital to traverse the ever-changing language instruction landscape successfully.

Furthermore, the future of linguistic education transcends traditional boundaries, embracing a lifelong learning perspective. Learning a new language is now more of a lifelong process that can take place in various contexts outside of conventional classrooms. Online language communities, language exchange programs, and virtual language meetups allow individuals to engage with native speakers and fellow learners globally. Being fluent in a language is more of a process than an endpoint; this trend toward continuous education reflects the fluid and ever-evolving character of language and communication.

As we gaze into the future of linguistic education, it is imperative to consider the role of technology not only in enhancing learning experiences and addressing the digital divide. Ensuring equitable access to technology and language learning resources is crucial to fostering inclusive linguistic education. Bridging the gap between those with access to advanced technology and those without is essential to prevent the exacerbation of existing inequalities in educational opportunities.

In conclusion, the future of linguistic education is marked by a convergence of technological innovation, pedagogical evolution, and a deepened understanding of the cultural dimensions of language. As we navigate this transformative landscape, embracing a holistic approach that combines technological advancements with effective pedagogy, cultural sensitivity, and a commitment to lifelong learning is essential. Linguistic education has great potential for the future in producing multilingual, culturally sensitive, adaptive, and successful citizens of our globalized and multicultural society.

# Chapter 9

# Beyond Language: Multimodal Communication

**Visual and Auditory Communication**

Communication, the bedrock of human interaction, has evolved through the ages. In the contemporary landscape, the symbiotic relationship between visual and auditory elements reshapes how we connect, convey, and comprehend information. Visual and auditory communication, once considered distinct entities, are now inseparable partners in the intricate dance of human expression. This essay delves into visual and auditory communication dynamics, exploring how these modalities intersect, complement each other, and contribute to the rich tapestry of our shared human experience.

With its roots deep in prehistoric cave paintings, visual communication has transcended the limitations of language and geography. In the digital age, the ubiquity of images, videos, and infographics has transformed how we consume information. From social media platforms to educational materials, visuals have become the currency of communication, transcending linguistic barriers and conveying complex ideas with remarkable clarity. The proliferation of visual storytelling has provided people and businesses with a potent medium for connecting with viewers on an emotional level and making an impression that will stay.

Moreover, visual communication extends beyond static images. The realm of motion pictures, animation, and virtual reality (VR) has initiated a new age in the world of dynamic visual experiences. Video content, in particular, has become a dominant force in online communication. Videos, including everything from vlogs to lessons, provide a multisensory experience by integrating images, audio, and text. This amalgamation of elements caters to diverse learning styles and creates a more immersive and memorable communication experience.

Simultaneously, auditory communication plays an equally crucial role in our daily interactions. Words, melodies, and soundscapes can make people feel something, show subtleties, and forge relationships. As a testament to the everlasting power of skillfully constructed spoken expression, the age-old practice of public speaking never fails to enthrall viewers. The complex web of the human face includes spoken words and non-verbal auditory clues like rhythm, intonation, and pitch.

The intersection of visual and auditory dialog is most evident in multimedia presentations. From business meetings to educational lectures, integrating visual aids and spoken words enhances comprehension and retention. Well-designed slides, infographics, and charts complement the spoken narrative, creating a synergistic effect that appeals to the visual and auditory senses. This convergence of modalities caters to diverse learning preferences and ensures a more comprehensive and engaging communication experience.

Audio content has never been more potent than in the digital era, with podcasts being a prime example. This audio-centric format's comeback reflects the universal need for narrative and storytelling. Listeners can engage in conversation, interviews, and reports on podcasts, which enable them to consume content even when they're not actively participating. By removing the limitations of sight, this audio experience creates a more personal and intimate relationship.

There has also been a considerable improvement in the quality of spoken communication due to the development of voice-enabled gadgets. In recent years, voice assistants, audiobooks, and voice commands on smart devices have become indispensable components of our everyday lives. Not only does the simplicity of connecting with electronics through voice make them more accessible, but it also reflects a more natural and intuitive manner of communication. The barriers between visual and audible communication are becoming increasingly blurry due to the ongoing improvement of technology, which gives an experience that is more integrated and seamless.

The fusion of visual and auditory elements in education has given rise to multimedia learning environments. Educational videos, interactive simulations, and virtual labs provide students with a holistic learning experience that engages their visual and auditory senses. This multimodal approach caters to diverse learning styles, accommodating students with varied preferences and abilities. The result is a more inclusive and practical educational experience beyond traditional methods.

Nevertheless, there are obstacles to overcome when combining visual and audio communication. Think carefully about the risks of distraction, information overload, and misunderstanding. The integrity of aural and visual content becomes paramount in this age of deepfakes and altered images. It underscores the importance of media literacy and critical thinking skills to navigate the complex information landscape and discern between genuine and manipulated communication.

In conclusion, visual and auditory communication dynamics reflect the evolving nature of human expression in the digital age. The convergence of these modalities has given rise to a rich tapestry of multimedia experiences that shape how we connect, learn, and communicate. As technology advances, the seamless integration of visual and auditory elements promises a more immersive and inclusive communication landscape, where the boundaries between these modalities dissolve, and the richness of human expression finds new avenues for exploration and innovation.

## Integrating Multimodal Approaches

In education and communication, the traditional reliance on singular modes of engagement is gradually giving way to a more inclusive and dynamic paradigm – that of multimodal approaches. This shift acknowledges the different ways in which individuals take in, process, and communicate information. It advocates for integrating various sensory modalities, including visual, aural, kinesthetic, and tactile components. By seamlessly blending these modes, educators, communicators, and content creators can cater to the varied learning preferences of their audiences, fostering a more comprehensive and practical experience.

When it comes to education, where students have varying cognitive styles and preferences, multimodal techniques are especially relevant because of the nature of the subject matter. Recognizing the significance of visual learning, educators are integrating multimedia elements into their teaching materials. Educational videos, infographics, and interactive simulations engage students visually, providing a dynamic supplement to traditional text-based instruction. The visual component enhances understanding and adds a layer of interest and excitement to the learning process. At the same time, auditory details, which include podcasts, discussions, and lectures, add to a more comprehensive learning experience by enabling students to take in knowledge through various channels.

The power of multimodal approaches is exemplified in the realm of technology-enhanced learning. Immersive learning environments are created by virtual reality (VR) and augmented reality (AR), which combine visual, audio, and frequently touch stimuli. Learners can investigate historical locations, carry out virtual experiments, or participate in simulated scenarios, all contributing to improved comprehension and recall. These technologies' interactive and multisensory nature accommodates different learning styles and promotes active engagement, transforming the learning experience into a participatory journey.

The significance of active participation in learning has been acknowledged by incorporating tactile and kinesthetic components into the educational process. Hands-on activities, experiments, and interactive projects allow students to apply theoretical knowledge in practical contexts. This experiential learning caters to kinesthetic learners and fosters a deeper understanding of concepts through active exploration and manipulation. By combining visual, auditory, kinesthetic, and tactile elements, educators create a multimodal learning environment that appeals to a spectrum of learners, enhancing inclusivity and effectiveness.

Not only is the education sector undergoing a transformation due to the adoption of multimodal approaches, but several businesses are also experiencing a transformation in their communication strategies. Multimedia campaigns, for example, are used in marketing and advertising to attract a wide variety of consumers by utilizing the power of graphics, audio, and interactive material. In terms of developing a narrative for a memorable and engaging brand, brands are aware of the need to appeal to customers through sensory experiences. This may be achieved using images, videos, music, and interactive aspects. A multimodal method offers a more resonant and engaging communication experience, and this approach acknowledges that individuals connect with information in various ways.

In the digital age, social media platforms epitomize integrating multimodal approaches. Posts like Instagram and TikTok combine images, videos, captions, and sometimes music, creating a multisensory user experience. These multimodal messages' succinct yet dynamic nature caters to online communication's fast-paced and visually oriented nature. Emoticons, gifs, and stickers further contribute to the multimodal language of digital communication, allowing individuals to convey emotions and expressions beyond text constraints.

The significance of multimodal approaches extends to professional settings, where effective communication is paramount. The use of visual aids, audio cues, and interactive components is beneficial in many contexts, including business presentations. To make their presentations more interesting and complex, presenters typically use visual aids like slideshows, movies, and infographics. Not only does this multimodal strategy boost audience understanding, but it also adds to the message's overall impact and persuasiveness.

Although it is clear that multimodal techniques have advantages, some problems must be overcome, notably about accessibility and inclusivity. Individuals with difficulties with vision or hearing may encounter obstacles while attempting to access particular modalities. Therefore, it is essential to design multimodal content with accessibility in mind, incorporating features such as closed captions, alternative text, and tactile options. Additionally, ensuring that content is culturally sensitive and does not rely on assumptions about users' preferences is crucial to creating an inclusive experience for diverse audiences.

In conclusion, incorporating multimodal techniques reflects a paradigm shift in how we approach communication and education. By recognizing and embracing the diversity of sensory modalities, we create environments that cater to individuals' varied preferences and needs. In the classroom, online, or in professional settings, the strength of mixing visual, aural, kinesthetic, and tactile elements rests in its capacity to create diversity, engagement, and a deeper grasp of the material. This is true regardless of the environment. As we navigate the future of education and communication, the seamless integration of multimodal approaches is a testament to our commitment to embrace diversity and enhance the richness of human experiences.

**Impact on Information Retrieval**

In the rapidly evolving information retrieval landscape, emerging technologies reshape how individuals' access, analyze, and make sense of vast data. With the advent of advanced algorithms, artificial intelligence (AI), and innovative search methodologies, the traditional information retrieval paradigms are transforming. This essay explores the multifaceted implications of these technological advancements, delving into how they influence the efficiency, accuracy, and user experience in information retrieval.

One of the pivotal changes in information retrieval is attributed to the advancements in AI, particularly machine learning algorithms. These algorithms, which are powered by enormous datasets, can learn and customize themselves, enabling them to perform searches that are more intelligent and aware of their context. To deliver personalized search results tailored to each individual's interests, machine learning models can recognize trends, user behavior, and the relevance of material. This level of customization enhances the user experience and contributes to more accurate and targeted information retrieval, aligning the search results with the specific needs and interests of users.

Moreover, natural language processing (NLP) has emerged as a game-changer in information retrieval. NLP allows systems to understand and interpret human language, enabling more nuanced and contextually relevant search queries. Conversational interfaces, chatbots, and voice-activated search engines leverage NLP to interact with users more naturally and intuitively. This shift towards more human-like interactions not only simplifies the search process but also broadens accessibility, allowing individuals with varying levels of technological proficiency to engage with information retrieval systems effortlessly.

Semantic search integration further exemplifies emerging technologies' impact on information retrieval. Unlike traditional keyword-based searches, semantic search seeks to understand the intent and meaning behind a query, considering the context and relationships between words. This approach enables more accurate and contextually relevant results by deciphering the user's underlying intentions. As a result, semantic search enhances the precision of information retrieval, reducing the likelihood of irrelevant or misleading search outcomes.

The advent of voice search represents a significant shift in how individuals interact with information retrieval systems. Enabled by advancements in speech recognition technology, voice search allows users to articulate queries verbally, mimicking natural conversation.

This mode of interaction caters to the growing preference for hands-free and on-the-go access to information. Voice search improves the user experience by delivering a more streamlined and user-friendly interface and necessitates modifications to content optimization tactics. This is because voiced inquiries frequently differ from their written equivalents.

When it comes to the recovery of visual information, computer vision technologies are playing a role that is becoming increasingly transformational. Image recognition algorithms can analyze visual content, allowing users to conduct searches based on images rather than text. It benefits the e-commerce, art, and design sectors, where visual aspects are important. This skill is essential in these fields. The integration of visual information retrieval not only expands the scope of search possibilities but also enhances information access efficiency, especially in scenarios where images convey more than words.

Additionally, the effect of developing technologies also impacts recommendation systems. Through collaborative filtering, machine learning algorithms thoroughly examine user behavior, preferences, and interactions to make recommendations for pertinent information. Whether in the context of streaming services, e-commerce platforms, or news aggregation, recommendation systems contribute to a more personalized and tailored information retrieval experience. By anticipating user preferences, these systems streamline the search process, presenting users with content that aligns with their interests and consumption patterns.

While the impact of emerging technologies on information retrieval is undoubtedly transformative, it is challenging. Concerns regarding privacy, algorithm bias, and the ethical implications of decision-making driven by artificial intelligence highlight the necessity of responsible and transparent implementation. Striking a balance between personalized user experiences and safeguarding privacy rights is critical as information retrieval systems evolve. Additionally, addressing biases in algorithms to ensure fair and unbiased search results remains an ongoing endeavor in pursuing ethical information retrieval practices.

In conclusion, the influence of new technologies on information retrieval is a profound and multifaceted transformation. From AI-driven algorithms and natural language processing to semantic search and visual recognition, these advancements are shaping a landscape where access to information is more intuitive, personalized, and contextually aware. As we navigate this evolving terrain, embracing the potential of these technologies while simultaneously addressing the ethical and privacy implications is imperative. The future of

information retrieval promises even greater efficiency, accuracy, and user-centric experiences, paving the way for a more interconnected and informed global society.

## Chapter 10

## Navigating the Uncharted Territory

**Challenges and Opportunities**

Throughout the ever-changing landscape of the 21st century, characterized by technological developments, cultural shifts, and global interconnection, individuals and organizations face various difficulties and opportunities. These dual facets, intricately woven into the fabric of our daily lives, shape the course of our collective journey. This section explores the dynamic interplay between challenges and opportunities, acknowledging the complexities that arise while recognizing the potential for growth, innovation, and positive transformation.

One of the most pressing problems facing modern society is the lightning-fast pace at which technical progress is made. While innovations in artificial intelligence, automation, and digital connectivity have revolutionized industries and daily routines, they have also given rise to concerns related to job displacement, ethical considerations, and the digital divide. As automation continues to reshape the workforce, the challenge lies in equipping individuals with the skills needed to thrive in a technology-driven era. Nevertheless, this difficulty presents an opportunity for efforts to reskill and upskill individuals, cultivating a culture that values continuous learning and adaptation throughout one's life.

Societal challenges, including inequality, diversity, and environmental sustainability, have become increasingly prominent globally. Addressing disparities in access to education, healthcare, and economic opportunities underscores the imperative for inclusive and equitable solutions. Amid these challenges, an opportunity for transformative change emerges, where individuals and institutions actively create more just and sustainable systems. Initiatives that promote diversity, inclusion, and sustainable practices can pave the way for a more harmonious coexistence with our planet and each other.

The problems brought about by global health crises, such as the COVID-19 pandemic, have brought to light the significance of being resilient and well-prepared in the healthcare field. The need for accessible and effective healthcare systems has become more evident than ever, with disparities in healthcare infrastructure and vaccine distribution accentuating existing challenges. Yet, within this crisis lies an opportunity to reimagine healthcare delivery, leverage telemedicine technologies, and strengthen global cooperation to ensure the health and well-being of all. As a result of the pandemic, there has been a recommitment to enhancing public health and accelerating the implementation of innovative solutions within the healthcare industry.

When it comes to adjusting to the requirements of a constantly shifting world, educational systems cannot meet the challenge. Traditional education models are being reconsidered in the face of digital transformation, with questions about the effectiveness of remote learning, the digital divide, and the need for personalized, lifelong learning experiences. However, within this challenge lies an opportunity to harness the potential of technology for inclusive and accessible education. Online learning platforms, adaptive learning tools, and collaborative digital resources offer new possibilities for democratizing education and catering to diverse learning styles.

Economic challenges, exacerbated by global uncertainties and geopolitical tensions, present formidable obstacles to sustainable development. Income inequality, unemployment, and economic instability demand innovative solutions. Nevertheless, these issues also give opportunities for rethinking economic structures, encouraging entrepreneurial endeavors, and embracing policies and procedures that are environmentally responsible. The push for a green economy, circular business models, and socially responsible investing exemplify a shift towards more sustainable and equitable economic practices.

The digital environment brings several difficulties relating to cybersecurity, data privacy, and misinformation despite providing unprecedented connectedness and access to information. The vulnerability of digital infrastructure to cyber threats and the ethical implications of data collection require vigilant attention. Simultaneously, these challenges provide an impetus for developing robust cybersecurity measures, establishing ethical frameworks for data use, and cultivating digital literacy skills. With its challenges and opportunities, the digital era underscores the importance of responsible technology use and governance.

Environmental deterioration negatively impacts ecosystems, livelihoods, and future generations' well-being, which has far-reaching effects. Nevertheless, this ecological crisis brings the possibility of taking action that may bring about transformation. There is a rising understanding of the interdependence between human activities and the earth's health, shown in the push for conservation measures, sustainable agricultural methods, and renewable fuels. The challenge of environmental sustainability calls for creative solutions that emphasize the delicate balance between the advancement of humanity and the ecosystem's overall health.

Social and political challenges, characterized by geopolitical tensions, polarization, and governance issues, underscore the complexity of navigating a globally interconnected world. The imperative for diplomatic dialogue, collaboration, and the promotion of democratic values becomes evident in the face of these challenges. However, within global affairs lies an opportunity for diplomatic breakthroughs, grassroots movements advocating for justice and equality, and strengthening international partnerships. The challenges posed by geopolitical uncertainties offer a platform for fostering unity, understanding, and collective action on a global scale.

In conclusion, the interplay between challenges and opportunities defines the narrative of our contemporary existence. The complexities inherent in technological, societal, economic, and environmental dynamics demand thoughtful and adaptive responses. Nevertheless, the possibility for invention, expansion, and constructive change may be found inside every obstacle. A future that is not just conscious of its complexities but also committed to exploiting them for the greater good may be shaped by embracing the opportunities that result from conquering problems. This not only helps to promote resilience but also pushes societal progress. As individuals, communities, and nations navigate this intricate web of challenges and opportunities, the collective pursuit of informed, ethical, and inclusive solutions becomes imperative for a sustainable and harmonious future.

## The Role of Society in Shaping Language Unleashed

Language, as a dynamic and living entity, is not confined to the realm of linguistics but is intricately woven into the fabric of society. The reciprocal relationship between language and culture is one of profound influence, where societal dynamics shape language and, in turn, language reflects and molds the collective identity of a community. This section delves into how society plays a pivotal role in shaping language, exploring the nuances of this symbiotic relationship that unleashes linguistic evolution and transformation.

A society's ideals, customs, and cultural nuances are reflected in the language that can be used to communicate. The lexicon of a language encapsulates the collective wisdom, beliefs, and lived experiences of a community. Through language, cultural identities find expression, with words, phrases, and idioms acting as vessels that carry the rich tapestry of shared history and traditions. As a result, language development is intricately connected with the ever-changing terrain of cultural views. This is because language acknowledges and adapts to the dynamic forces that shape the collective consciousness.

Societal changes, marked by shifts in technology, politics, and social structures, profoundly impact language. The rapid advancement of technology, for instance, introduces new concepts, terms, and expressions that find their way into everyday discourse. The emergence of the digital age has birthed a lexicon of emojis, hashtags, and internet slang that reflects the interconnected, fast-paced nature of contemporary society. Moreover, political and social movements bring about linguistic shifts, with terms such as "woke," "cancel culture," and "intersectionality" entering mainstream discourse as society grapples with evolving perspectives on justice, equity, and identity.

One of the most powerful tools that may be used is the language used to promote social inclusion and cohesiveness. The choice of words and expressions can foster unity or perpetuate division within a society. Inclusivity in language becomes crucial in acknowledging diverse identities, experiences, and perspectives. For example, the evolution of gender-inclusive language reflects a societal commitment to recognizing and respecting diverse gender identities. Language, when wielded with sensitivity, has the potential to dismantle stereotypes, challenge prejudices, and pave the way for a more inclusive and equitable society.

The role of society in shaping language extends to the realm of linguistic norms and standards. Normative effects determine what is considered acceptable or unacceptable within a particular group and can affect language because language is a social construct. Linguistic prescriptivism, often influenced by institutions such as academia, media, and governance, establishes rules and standards that guide language use. However, societal upheavals, driven by cultural movements and grassroots action, challenge linguistic conventions. This, in turn, prompts arguments regarding language inclusion, linguistic variety, and the recognition of marginalized linguistic variations.

The impact of globalization on language underscores the interconnectedness of societies in the contemporary world. As borders blur and cultures intermingle, languages undergo transformations that reflect this global exchange. Loanwords, borrowings, and code-switching become linguistic phenomena that mirror the multicultural tapestry of societies. The emergence of global lingua francas, such as English and Mandarin, further highlights the role of culture in shaping languages that transcend national boundaries, facilitating communication worldwide.

Slang and informal language, often dismissed as deviations from linguistic norms, play a crucial role in capturing the spirit and ethos of societal subcultures. Youth cultures, in particular, contribute to linguistic innovation by creating slang, jargon, and expressions that define their social identities. The wider society's adoption of such informal language illustrates the porous nature of linguistic boundaries and the constant interplay between societal dynamics and linguistic evolution.

In the digital age, social media platforms amplify the impact of society on language, providing a virtual space where linguistic trends emerge, spread, and evolve rapidly. Hashtags, memes, and viral phrases become linguistic phenomena that encapsulate societal sentiments, shared experiences, and cultural moments. The democratization of language through online spaces empowers individuals and communities to contribute to linguistic evolution, challenging traditional language usage and dissemination hierarchies.

Language, as a vehicle for power and persuasion, is wielded by societal institutions to influence public discourse and perception. The construction of narratives, the transmission of ideologies, and the establishment of norms are all processes controlled by the media, political bodies, and educational institutions. The power dynamics embedded in language use become evident in the framing of issues, the selection of words, and the perpetuation of certain linguistic conventions. The scrutiny of language by critical discourse analysis unveils the subtle ways societal power structures are reinforced or challenged through linguistic choices.

The interaction between society and language is a dynamic interplay that unleashes ongoing change, adaptation, and transformation. In conclusion, this relationship is quite busy. Shifts in culture advances in technology, political movements, and the dynamics of inclusion and exclusion all contribute to the formation of language in society.

At the same time, language, as a powerful tool of expression, reflects societal values, constructs identities, and influences perceptions. As organizations navigate the complexities of the contemporary world, the role of language remains a profound force that both mirrors and molds the collective consciousness, contributing to the ever-unfolding narrative of human civilization.

## Envisioning the Next Phase of Linguistic Evolution

The evolution of language, an ever-unfolding tapestry woven by the intricacies of human communication, continues to adapt and transform in response to the dynamic forces of the contemporary world. As we stand at the precipice of a new era marked by technological advancements, societal shifts, and global interconnectedness, envisioning the next phase of linguistic evolution becomes a compelling exploration of the possibilities. This section dives into the multiple facets of linguistic development, examining the influence of emerging technology, the impact of cultural and socioeconomic dynamics, and the different routes through which language may transform.

One of the defining elements of the next phase of linguistic evolution is the pervasive influence of technology. The digital age, characterized by instant connectivity and information dissemination, has ushered in many linguistic innovations. Conversational agents, language translation algorithms, and voice-activated assistants are not only causing a shift in how we communicate, but they are also contributing to the standardization of linguistic landscapes around the world. The intersection of technology and language promises a future where communication barriers are dismantled, fostering a more interconnected and linguistically diverse world.

In addition, the development of technology that enables virtual and augmented reality has brought about new opportunities for the evolution of language. As virtual spaces integrate into our daily experiences, language may transcend traditional written and spoken forms, incorporating immersive and interactive elements. Creating a new lexicon that includes words that are accompanied by visual, auditory, and tactile components, generating a multimodal language experience, could be made possible through virtual environments, simulations, and programs that provide augmented reality. Integrating these technologies can redefine how we conceptualize and engage with language in personal and professional contexts.

The influence of cultural and societal dynamics on linguistic evolution is poised to intensify in the next phase. As societies become more interconnected, diverse, and aware of global interdependence, languages will continue to borrow, adapt, and evolve through cultural exchange. The emergence of new terminologies and linguistic expressions reflective of contemporary societal norms, values, and challenges will become a hallmark of linguistic evolution. The ongoing conversation around inclusivity and recognition of marginalized voices may lead to a more conscious and deliberate development of language, fostering representative linguistic landscapes that reflect the diversity within societies.

Furthermore, the next phase of linguistic evolution may witness a reevaluation of linguistic norms and standards. The democratization of language through digital platforms, social media, and online communities empowers individuals to shape linguistic conventions. Non-traditional linguistic forms, such as emojis, memes, and internet slang, are already challenging conventional norms, providing alternative modes of expression and communication. This democratization invites a more inclusive approach to linguistic evolution, where linguistic diversity and variation are embraced rather than marginalized.

Language, as a tool of power and influence, is subject to shifts in political and ideological landscapes. During the subsequent stage of linguistic evolution, the negotiation of inherent power dynamics in language use may occur. Sociopolitical movements advocating for linguistic inclusivity, language rights, and the recognition of linguistic diversity may gain momentum, challenging linguistic hegemony and promoting equitable representation. The mention of diverse linguistic varieties, dialects, and linguistic heritage becomes imperative in envisioning a future where language is a vehicle for empowerment rather than marginalization.

The integration of technology into education, coupled with a growing awareness of diverse learning styles, will impact how languages are taught and acquired. Adaptive learning technologies, language apps, and online resources may redefine language education, making it more personalized, accessible, and effective. The emphasis on multilingualism and the cultivation of linguistic competencies may become central to educational curricula, reflecting a global perspective that values linguistic diversity as an asset.

Language evolution is inextricably linked to the changing nature of work and professional communication. The globalization of industries and the rise of remote work have necessitated effective cross-cultural communication, leading to the adaptation of linguistic conventions in professional settings. The future may witness the emergence of new workplace linguistic norms that prioritize clarity, inclusivity, and cultural sensitivity. Moreover, integrating AI-driven language technologies in professional communication may redefine how individuals professionally engage with written and spoken language.

While envisioning the next phase of linguistic evolution holds promise and excitement, it is challenging. The use of artificial intelligence in language generation raises several complicated questions that require careful study to be navigated. Concerns regarding linguistic hegemony and ethical problems regarding the introduction of artificial intelligence into the process of language generation are among these subjects. To shape a future in which linguistic evolution is progressive and inclusive, it is essential to find a way to strike a balance between the advancement of technology and the preservation of linguistic heritage, as well as between global connectedness and local linguistic identities.

In conclusion, the next phase of linguistic evolution stands at the intersection of technology, culture, society, and education. The potential for transformative changes in how we communicate, the emergence of new linguistic expressions, and the reevaluation of linguistic norms mark a future that is both dynamic and full of possibilities. Embracing linguistic evolution in this era requires a collective and informed approach that acknowledges technology's impact, celebrates linguistic diversity, and fosters inclusive linguistic practices. As language continues its journey of evolution, it remains a testament to the adaptive and creative nature of human communication, forever responsive to the evolving needs and dynamics of our interconnected world.

# Conclusion

In conclusion, "Language Unleashed: Unveiling the Future of Communication and Information Retrieval" surpasses the confines of conventional linguistic inquiry, allowing readers a thrilling excursion into the unknown areas of language evolution. Throughout the e-book, we've unraveled the intricacies of technological advancements and emerging trends that redefine how we communicate and retrieve information.

As the final pages unfold, it becomes evident that the future of language is not just a distant concept but a dynamic force shaping our daily interactions. The e-book has successfully woven together the threads of linguistic theory, technological innovation, and real-world applications, presenting a comprehensive understanding of how language is unleashed in this digital era.

One key takeaway is the interconnectedness of language and technology, where artificial intelligence, machine learning, and innovative communication tools converge to redefine the very fabric of human expression. The e-book prompts us to reflect on the adaptability required to thrive in this linguistic landscape, where traditional communication methods undergo a metamorphosis into something more nuanced, efficient, and interconnected.

Furthermore, "Language Unleashed" is a call to action, more specifically, an invitation to use the opportunities given by this revolution in language. It challenges us to actively participate in shaping the linguistic future, urging readers to harness the power of emerging technologies for effective communication and information retrieval. The insights from this exploration empower individuals, educators, and professionals alike to navigate the evolving landscape confidently and critically.

As we bid farewell to the pages of "Language Unleashed," we carry a profound awareness of the transformative potential within our grasp. The e-book serves not only as a guide to the future of language but as a catalyst for innovation, pushing boundaries, and inspiring a new era of communication. The journey does not end here; instead, it marks the beginning of a continuous exploration, where language is genuinely unleashed, and the future beckons with endless possibilities.

*Thank you for buying and reading/listening to our book. If you found this book useful/helpful please take a few minutes and leave a review on the platform where you purchased our book. Your feedback matters greatly to us.*

www.ingramcontent.com/pod-product-compliance
Lightning Source LLC
LaVergne TN
LVHW021825060526
838201LV00058B/3512